My Swan Song

by
Myra Chave-Jones

Galactic Publishers Limited.

Roxeth House
Shaftesbury Avenue
Harrow
Middlesex
HA2 0PZ

w: http://www.galacticpublishers.net/

First published in Great Britain in 2010.

Text Copyright © Myra Chave-Jones 2010.

Pictorial Copyright © Galactic Publishers Limited 2010.

ISBN 978-1-907665-13-4

Typeset by Galactic Publishers Limited, Harrow, Middlesex.

CONTENTS PAGE

PREFACE

Myra and I have known each other since we were students at Cambridge, and we have forged a long and enduring friendship.

I have always appreciated how Myra has developed her understanding of our human experience, especially within her pioneering work within the organisation known as Care and Counsel.

Her varied experiences will help many people who read this little book.

I wish it well as it goes on its journey.

Rev. Dr. John Stott CBE

FOREWORD

With an ageing population there is probably no more important topic to talk about than growing old and facing death, and surely the best guide to these desperately neglected issues is someone who has earned the right to comment—someone having extended years—possessing waning strength and painfully aware that their days on this earth are limited.

I recommend this book to you with both sorrow and pleasure. Sorrow, because Myra is an old friend who inspired me over thirty years ago when we first met; and pleasure because of the riches of wisdom that she has given us in these few pages.

Myra has walked on the road of ageing and illness that, in due time, most of us will walk. This is an honest and wise account of what we may face, uncoloured by false hopes and wishful thinking. Lest you be concerned, let me reassure you, this book is devoid of the self-pity, regrets or grumpiness that you might fear. Instead there is an unflinching recounting of fears, pains and disappointments, with a courageous gaze at what lies ahead, and most precious of all, a rich and deep hope for what lies beyond. This is a book to be read, re-read, cherished and shared.

Myra has entitled this little book 'My Swan Song'. It is worth remembering the story behind the words: Swan Song, is the ancient (and quite false) belief that the Mute Swan never sings—during its lifetime—until just before it dies when it sings one last beautiful song. This book is indeed a song and it is beautiful.

Myra, you have helped many through your previous books. I believe that you will help many more through this your final volume.

J. John (Canon)

INTRODUCTION

I was born almost 87 years ago in the days of strict Victorian parents, when children should be seen and not heard. One of the biggest regrets of my life is that I was never a mother, but on reflection, it is probably just as well. I would have made a horrible one!

At the time when I had to choose between marriage and a career (there was no other alternative in those days), I chose my fascinating career. The thought of a host of screaming kids all round my feet, was a complete turn-off.

It was only much later, when I began my training in the world of psychotherapy, that things turned upside down for me. Two of the first things that I discovered were that you don't have to be good to be loved, and that even the youngest baby in the family is as important as everyone else. Obvious really, but at the time it was mind-blowing to me.

So, now I am addicted to small children, especially if they belong to other people! To see them toddling along the street, holding an adult's hand in such trustful safety, makes me stop, watch and wonder.

Perhaps I have been a different sort of mother to a lot of people. Without mothering them, I have stood alongside many, while they wrestled with deep internal problems, which were blighting their lives. I have endeavoured to help people to see *for themselves* the causes of some of the problems that they were facing and assist them to look for the changes needed. There was often the pain of change and the re-establishment of trust and love. This was hard work for all concerned. In my experience miracles don't always happen instantaneously; it sometimes takes a long time, but, when they do, it is well worth the effort of patience and perseverance—and prayer. The joy of a life transformed and changed is almost indescribable.

Eventually, the time for my own retirement came. I had a few years of freedom (i.e. more room for choices) in store, until I was suddenly and unexpectedly catapulted into the world of illness and old age—and the rest is history. The amazing thing is, on two separate occasions, my doctors have indicated that they did not expect to see me again. Nevertheless, I am, still here but, I have to add, with some reluctance. I find that I am becoming very tired of this body as it will not do as it is told anymore. People tell me how well I look, and that is nice in a way, but I don't always feel very nice! However, while I am still alive, I am trying to be as comforting and as helpful to other people who have much worse problems than I have—until I finally go to my heavenly home!

So many people have contributed anonymously to this, my little song, so much so that I have lost count of the individuals.

Most of the anecdotes have been offered by anonymous friends, who did not even realise that they were making a particular contribution as they shared in my journey.

I am specially grateful for all the skill, expertise and patience of Peter Cockburn—who rescued me from computer disaster several times. I also wish to thank my friend Geoff Marshall-Taylor, and for all of his knowledge and craft with words (not to mention his tireless patience). There are many others, who have made some solid contributions with their time and ideas and I owe them all a big debt of gratitude.

My special thanks go to my editor and publisher, Arwyn Bailey, whose enthusiasm and encouragement made this happen.

Myra Chave-Jones

INTRODUCTION: a postscript

I felt that I must add to the kind comments of others regarding Myra. As soon as we were sent the manuscript and draft of this book, I could not put it down. I read it in one sitting. Then I read the draft again, but far more slowly, taking the time to absorb the snippets of logic, truth and the beauty of the words in front of me.

I felt that I must meet Myra and I wasted no time in arranging a meeting. I was not disappointed. I found a humble soul who had a razor sharp wit, yet she maintains a perspective on life that many of us would wish to gain, but very few of us manage to achieve.

I consider it to be a privilege to be asked to publish this small volume, that is packed to the brim with so much wisdom and treasure. My own sorrow is that I have only just met Myra, but my hope is that this book will be a lasting legacy to a remarkable lady.

Arwyn Bailey

(Writer and Director of Galactic Publishers)

PREAMBLE

How old is old? The well known author and broadcaster, John Humphrys is said to have commented:

> You know that you are old when you bend down to tie your shoe laces and wonder what else you could be doing while you are down there!

Of course, so much depends upon our own personal circumstances and things like our physical health and even the weather! The stresses of our life such as work, finance, relationships, physical disability or any of the other many ills that flesh is heir too can weigh us down and take the sparkle out of life. We are well aware that you are as old as you feel!

But for our purposes at the moment, I have in mind people who are not likely to see mid-eighty again, roughly. Old age seems to make us change and people sometimes write us off as being past it. We are thought not know much about anything. We are sometimes tempted to think that about ourselves. I would like to invite you now to come with me, if you would like to, on an exploration of some aspects of old age that often escape people's attention.

Sometimes we decide it is time to get rid of some of our old papers and other rubbish that we may have accumulated over the years. The trouble is that as we start to examine our old files, photographs and stuff, and as we begin to read these old letters and musings, and as we look at images of the past, once again we travel down memory lane and we can't bear to tear up some precious parts of our past life. So back goes all this old junk which may mean little to anyone else. But we have just had a good laugh, or cry, for an hour or so.

The other day I was turning out some old things and came across a book of photographs of my own 80th birthday celebrations. What a happy and love-filled day it was—even the sun shone brightly! The only shadow over the day was the absence of six of my life-long friends, all of whom were either too ill, or too old, to travel. Little did I realise that this same shadow would lengthen to extremely painful proportions before I was very much older.

This darkness began with the death of four of those life-long friends within just three months of one another. For me, it felt as though four great cedar trees had been felled from my landscape, leaving a gaping hole and emptiness. I'm sure you know what that feels like to see those that you love pass from this transitory life. The Good Book says:

> ...we finish our days with a moan. The length of our days is seventy years, or eighty, if we have the strength; yet their span is but trouble and sorrow, for they quickly pass and we fly away.[1]

This seems true enough! Some days are more moanful than others but there continue to be days of quiet joy.

Just in case you had not realised, I have just quoted from the Holy Bible, which is full of truths and life experience. I am a committed Christian and I have found much consolation, earthy wisdom and encouragement in the Bible. I realise that not everyone who may be reading this will have the same outlook as me, but, whatever our Christian or religious persuasion (or lack of it) might be, we all share the same potential future—old age and flying away.

The foundation upon which our life is built vitally affects the way in which we might cope with the vicissitudes and losses that we encounter on our pathway of life, and the prospect of death, that lies ahead.

---

[1] From the book of Psalms, Chapter 90 verses 9 - 10.

One reason for my putting pen to paper is that most of the people who write about old age are not themselves seriously old. The poet, John Keats, is reputed to have said, very wisely, that:

Nothing ever becomes real until it has been experienced.[2]

The perspective of someone who is still middle-aged is bound to be somewhat different from that of somebody who is in the thick of old age! Some of the content of this manuscript might appear boring and incomprehensible to those who are viewing old age from a distance, but at times that is just what old age does feel like—boring and incomprehensible! In contrast, it must also be acknowledged that old age can be interesting and very challenging at times. You have to be very old to know just what it feels like. You may know a lot about it but you have to experience it to understand it. It's like playing football—or marriage—until you actually do it personally, you cannot fully appreciate all that goes into it.

The second reason for these musings on life, is that for a really old person (like me) to summon up the required amount of energy and interest to write is a bit unusual, I gather. Perhaps, in this case, putting my observations into writing is more a piece of personal therapy and a process of self indulgent clarification, rather than some account of a new and profound discovery. I am not attempting to say anything startlingly new, we are all too aware of the general problems that are involved in old age. This not a how to do it guide or manual; it is more of a this is what it feels like account. This maybe some sort of comfort to people who live alone, or who have not had much contact with other people in this stage of life previously.

I am also told that people are not interested in the subject of old age,

<hr>

[2] From a letter by John Keats to his brother and sister-in-law, George and Georgiana Keats, 1819.

but I question this. Certainly, for the very young, the subject is irrelevant and unattractive. It does not usually appear on their landscape. For the people in their fifties, the subject can become very relevant if they find themselves having to care for their elderly parents who can no longer manage on their own. This can become a massive problem for the middle aged who are being pulled in three emotional directions at the same time as they have a duty to give attention and care to their own adult children, grandchildren and elderly parents.

Also, the fact that so much advertising concentrates on the desirability of looking young and agile, indicates a great fear of the damage that age can do to an attractive body.

By way of introducing myself I should explain that in my seventies I was indeed fairly alert and quite sprightly. On one occasion I went to look at a retirement village thinking that I might have need of such a place one day in the distant future—I was feeling a bit fragile after a recent replacement to my second hip. It was a lovely sunny morning, the trees were beautiful and the flowers rich and colourful. The first sight that greeted me was a very old couple, one using a walking stick and the other with a zimmer frame, coming towards me.

Oh dear, I pondered, I wouldn't like to be surrounded by people like that. The village itself seems to be pleasant enough—but oh dear, the thought of all of those old people!

Please excuse my arrogance. I had no real experience, and I did not understand, let alone appreciate, those who were a decade or so older than myself. So I sailed into my eighties blithely unaware of what I was about to encounter just ahead. I ended up living in a different retirement village that was, and continues to be, full of people whom are labelled as old. But contrary to my initial thoughts, and my abject horror, I have found fellow human beings who have lived interesting and varied lives. Many of them are good fun and friendly, and there is much kindness and warmth about the place, and we help each other when necessary.

Our lives are occasionally tinged with sadness when one of the residents shuffles off this mortal coil. We are a relatively cheerful and ordinary microcosm of the world in general, including a dose of village gossip that wars are often made of!

I am now requiring the use of a walking stick or two, and I am trying to cope reasonably well with the inevitable limitations of illness and the advancing years. Some of us are growing more bent and have increasing physical problems, which means that we have to cope with life very differently from those of a younger disposition.

Four years ago I had had an operation. My good friend came with me to the hospital when the chilling diagnosis was confirmed—I had contracted malignant cancer.

As she drove home, my friend was sensitive enough to maintain complete silence. I sat there pulverised. Thoughts raced through my mind. This sort of thing happens to other people but not to me!

The surgeon had recommended an operation which had encouragingly been described as being very complicated and far too major a procedure to be carried out on people such as myself, normally, but my doctors thought that I looked a healthy enough specimen to take the risk. At least, that was what she said to me.

Afterwards, I realised that the only alternative would have been a very painful death within a short period of time. I had to have a pacemaker implanted before they would consider treatment of any sort. After sundry delays, regarding the pacemaker, I had to undergo a short but very intensive course of radiotherapy. At first, I wondered why people could sometimes be heard to be making a fuss about radiotherapy treatment, until I began to feel its after effects myself. Now, I have the utmost sympathy! Then came the surgery. I will spare you the gory details—suffice it to say that a good hospital was somewhat spoilt by the acute shortage of nursing staff. There was very little TLC about the place.

A year later, as predicted, I began to recognise the person that I used to be—but with significant differences! One of the huge differences is that in hospital I had experienced what seemed like a personal encounter with God.

In my utter, total helplessness and distress, I called on God for some sort of relief. I seemed to hear a little voice in my ear saying:

> But you aren't leaving much space for me in all this, are you? It's all too much for you and you can't manage it on your own.

Of course, being a decent upright Christian, I had always known and believed in my head that God loved and cared for me, but now I was to experience in my own heart and life what that really meant. Whenever I found myself thinking that it would be far easier to die, rather than continue living, there came a specific piece of comfort which was incredibly tailor-made to meet my need. Coincidence, of course—but coincidences do not happen several times a day, for several days in succession as they did for me. I could not deny that somebody was looking after me, and that that somebody knew my situation, in detail. This gave me food for thought.

For instance, on one particularly difficult day, a kindly adjacent patient brought over three copies of the magazine called Hello, to help the day along. I had not read of this periodical before, but in acknowledgement of her sympathy and kindness I began to look at them.

I saw a plethora of must-haves, and I could look into the lives of several apparently glamorous celebs, who were now into their third, or even fourth marriage, with several children in tow, all fathered by different men. This was combined with advice on how to look glamorous in fabulous clothes. There were even answers and advice on how to be successful in sexual encounters! Essential must have equipment for the kitchen was listed. Parental advice along with its inherent problems was freely given. The lifestyle advice seemed endless. Somehow, I did not find any of this very comforting, but it was exactly what I needed at that moment! The banal took my mind off my own distress and I did wonder how these celebrities react in the difficult circumstances of reality.

Had I been offered something more serious and edifying, I would not have been in a fit state to receive it. As I was giving the three copies of Hello back to my new friend, I was thinking about what I had that could be more comforting. One of my dear friends had sent me a book to read during the time I was in hospital. It was a gentle and very comforting journey through the famous 23rd Psalm that is entitled: Song of the Shepherd.[3] That book was an absolute lifeline for me during all of those difficult months. Such a well-known Psalm, but the writer of the book highlighted things that I had never noticed before.

All of this might be a very familiar experience to many, I am sketching the outline to assure you that I do know just a bit about the problems of pain and ageing, especially now that my previous active lifestyle has undergone such a dramatic change.

Perhaps I should add an apology here. I have not, as yet, had to experience the social problems of accommodation, acute financial

---

[3] Song of the Shepherd is by Tony Horsfall and was published by BRIF in 2004.

difficulty, or isolation, which make the problems of old age so very much more difficult to endure. So, although most of what I have noted is common to us all, there are serious omissions.

Here is the 23rd Psalm, with all of the imagery that would have been so familiar to Judean shepherds:

> The LORD is my shepherd, I shall not be in want.
>
> He makes me lie down in green pastures,
>
> he leads me beside quiet waters,
>
> he restores my soul.
>
> He guides me in paths of righteousness
>
> for his name's sake.
>
> Even though I walk
>
> through the valley of the shadow of death,
>
> I will fear no evil,
>
> for you are with me;
>
> your rod and your staff,
>
> they comfort me.
>
> You prepare a table before me
>
> in the presence of my enemies.
>
> You anoint my head with oil;
>
> my cup overflows.
>
> Surely goodness and love will follow me
>
> all the days of my life,
>
> and I will dwell in the house of the LORD
>
> forever.[4]

---

[4] From the book of Psalms, Chapter 23 verses 1 - 6.

LEARNING CURVES

When we were young we used to think people of sixty were tremendously old. Then suddenly, it became average for people to live until they were seventy. And now eighty has become an age that is normal. Many more of us live to be a venerable ninety. Shops are now beginning to sell congratulation cards for people who attain the mighty one hundred. Nowadays, we read the obituaries in the newspapers with great interest. Someone who has sadly died at seventy, seems to have been cut off in their prime.

What huge changes in our society and culture have taken place and swept through our world in the last century! Some of us can remember the days when there were few telephones, no television, and policemen used to stand at the centre of main crossroads wearing their white gloves, waving on the traffic or stopping it. It was safe to have the front door unlocked because no-one would break in, or to leave one's bike unlocked by the railings, knowing that it would be there when we got back. The postman would call two or three times a day and the milkman brought his churn to the door to fill our jugs with his various copper cylindrical ladles. The greengrocer used to come and ply his produce round the streets with his horse and cart, laden with fresh vegetables and fruit, and people used to collect the manure for their roses. We had roaring coal fires which heated half the room and left the far corners freezing. The washing was carried out in an outhouse over a live copper fire, then squeezed through a mangle or rubbed up and down on a dolly. If you wanted to cross the road you just took your life in your hands and hoped for the best. Of course there weren't many cars, but you might have been trampled by a horse! Then, as more cars began to appear, a clever Jewish gentleman invented black and white crossing places with flashing beacons, guiding you to a place where a pedestrian would have priority and, hopefully, safety. This gentleman's name was Horeb Elisha (hence the rather descriptive words: Belisha Beacon). If you can remember, like me, all, or any, of this then you are genuinely entitled to call yourself old.

How things have changed! Our parents would not know how to live in today's world. We hardly know ourselves, what with all the incredible electronic technology that has arrived on the scene.

To say that you are as old as you feel, seems almost tantamount to saying how long's a piece of string? But maybe, there is a good deal of truth in what we feel like. It is hard to be sprightly and busy if our poor body is screwed up with constant pain or adversely affected with some greatly debilitating illness, even though we might be in our prime chronologically speaking. A friend of mine said to me recently:

I think I know what it feels like to be old.

She was in her late thirties when for two years she was incapacitated by that mysterious illness M.E. (commonly known as Muscular Exhaustion). She explained that she was tired all of the time; and she had no strength to do her teaching job; she had a continuous cloud in her head so that she couldn't think clearly—she knew what she wanted to say but she couldn't get the words out. All this made for a very debilitating lack of self-confidence. She just felt old and useless.

On the other hand we often meet people who, in spite of their great age, appear to be marvellous, in that they look very active and involved in life. Presumably a lot depends upon their life experiences and their genes.

Life is full of learning curves; some of which are very steep. But I think that the steepest of all is about learning to grow old, and if possible, with some degree of grace.

LEARNING CURVES: childhood

This is obviously the first and perhaps one of the most important stages of our lives. It is crammed with new experiences, daily.

First of all, there is the traumatic introduction into the world, with all the pushing, squeezing and struggling. Infants have no notion of the love, preparations and excitement which, hopefully, will have accompanied them throughout all the long months of waiting, though doubtless they have had some experience of the various noises, conditions and movements which have more recently beset them.

What a startling and dramatic change all of those bright lights, loud noises, the feel of warm blankets and the blurred sight of human faces presents! No wonder their first instinct is to cry! Never mind the theory about needing to fill their lungs with air. And then, each day brings new experiences as they learn about the essentials of living their own small life. Although they maybe so defenceless, they soon discover that they have, within their power an unfailing resource. They possess a piercing and continuous cry which produces results! We see, on our televisions, some tragic results of extreme intolerance on the part of supposedly caring adults. Mercifully, this is not the norm, but the repeated nature of the parents' reactions to the distress signal of an infant, be it positive or negative, will influence, to some extent, the rest of their child's life. If these reactions are usually rough and impatient they will begin to be afraid to put out roots of love and trust; they will withdraw into self, although their persistent crying may lessen. On the other hand, if they experience gentle firmness and consistent sensitive care, they will begin to understand about safety in relationships.

They grow at a great rate, both emotionally and physically, and as time passes they discover that their legs were made to stand on and that hands can do many interesting things, and, despite all of the knocks and bruises that are part of the fun of finding out limitations of self and what makes things happen, they continue to explore and adventure into new areas of discovery.

There is something that is inherently adorable about the innocent, trusting face of a small child.

Then comes the day when they have to venture out to nursery, or the reception class at school. Their mother stands there watching the first of her precious offspring disappearing into the great unknown, and she tries hard to control her emotions as she sees the bewildered little face, and her child's tears, just like her own, are not far away. It is perhaps the first encounter with the ogre of separation. A nasty steep learning curve for such a little person.

Incidentally, it is interesting to note that in our old age it is easier to recall the events, places and sayings of our childhood than what happened yesterday. How important those childhood foundations are and how very deeply they become embedded in our unconscious mind. An emotionally healthy child needs to be sure of being loved, accepted and belonging to their family, and to discover their own identity. This environment leads to an appropriate sense of self-confidence.

As they grow older, this firm foundation will make it somewhat easier for them to win, or lose in life's difficulties. Struggles continue to go on from childhood, and through to old age. It is so much more comfortable to be able to retain a relatively calm depth of genuine equanimity in these circumstances, if the foundations have been laid securely.

LEARNING CURVES: adolescence

Here is the next major learning curve. This can be a difficult time for the individual and sometimes, the repercussions throughout the family can be very uncomfortable! What happened to that adorable little child? The body is undergoing some big changes and emotions that are hard to understand too often go out of control. What is happening? Who am I now? Where do I fit in? What are the rules now; if there are any, and who makes them? The peer pressure is very heavy and I am often very confused. I hate myself and everyone! Which university? What am I going to do with my life? There are such big decisions to be made!

These are the same basic questions that confront us all when a new phase of life begins to dawn but with adolescence the huge difference taking place is the new ability to create another human being. Sex becomes a priority concern. But this new power is for fun and for experimentation, they say, and the fearful responsibility of procreation falls out of serious reckoning.

There is also the use of drugs and other activities which are intended to add some spice to life, or they dull the emotional pain of alienation, meaningless and isolation. Peer pressure can present a formidable problem for the young, especially those who do not have a very stable home background. We see daily examples of groups of disaffected young people. They have no basic family structure and although they may not have much affection for each other there seems to be some safety in belonging to a gang. They can vent their inner meaninglessness and anger on any person—or property—that they choose or that crosses their path. They have never experienced what true love, trust and faithfulness are about.

In contrast it is delightful to see so many strong and energetic young people who have a very positive attitude to life and they engage in all sorts of goals and useful pursuits. We, oldies, often find ourselves looking at them with a sort of admiration, perhaps tinged with envy, until we remember that we were once like that, with equal amounts of vitality, energy, and ambitions—but that was a long time ago now!

LEARNING CURVES: marriage and parenthood

After a few more years of learning something about the intricacies of life, the journey leads us towards marriage—although nowadays people often seems to get things back to front and the wedding ceremony looks more like an excuse for an expensive party after several years of living together!

Adjusting to living in intimacy with another person brings many of the same old questions back again. Where are the boundaries? How do 1 handle the pain of really honest communication, so that conflict can become constructive rather than destructive? What happens when 1 can't get my own way? Is it always the same person who is the first to apologise? And so much more, if a balanced, satisfying relationship is to be established.

When the children come along the whole dynamic balance between the couple changes—a new lifestyle emerges with its joys and difficulties. Another learning curve has come with parenthood. The self-sacrifice required is a pleasure, but it is often costly, and not solely in the financial sense of the word. We cannot just carry on as before, treating this new human being as an additional piece of luggage!

Children of any age, but especially small infants, need the security of loving and trusted person who is able to hold them, sometimes physically and often emotionally. When their furious emotions feel desperate they need to be contained by an adult who will not be frightened, paralysed or overcome by them. Someone is required who will understand how terrifying that they can be to the infant. We can see, by the red screaming face and the flailing limbs how intense and total these emotions are within a child. The new infant has no previous experience that lost things can be found, or that pain can be relieved. For a little child, anything that has gone wrong is like the end of the world. The intensity in levels of fear, anger and frustration increase and it requires a good deal of intelligence, and insight, to be one step ahead of the situation most of the time.

How is a woman who has spent years of hard work training in her profession, meant to come to grips with the fact that being a full-time mother is the most important career that there is, for which she has probably had little or no training? How is she to balance her professional ambitions with the emotional needs of her vulnerable small child which involves much more than the physical care which anyone can give? Being a full-time mother may not be very glamorous, or lucrative, and it is certainly very hard work, with no holidays! Growing another human being is a serious business!

And as the years pass methods have to change, too. Teenagers have their violent emotions, as we know, and they, too, need to be held. Recently, a friend said to me with considerable emotion—at the end of years of trying to work out how to control helpfully:

> I am now learning to be a consulting mother to my teenagers rather than a controlling mother!

LEARNING CURVES: middle age

Familiar sorts of questions arise up within us—and not for the first time. What is the purpose of life? There are changes in priorities and in levels of energy, of satisfaction, and some uncertainty about one's value in society. We may be tempted to start looking around for pastures that appear to be greener. The children are leaving home and what about my own, or our own, future? Both husband and wife have grown more mature and changed in many ways and now we begin to hear the familiar refrain of, 'You aren't the person that I married;' or yet another sad refrain of, 'I never really knew what love was before I met...' Of course, it is not always like this. Middle age should be embraced wholeheartedly, as it is often an opportunity to deepen the marriage relationship when there are less pressures in the family.

It is a bit staggering to discover that in one's forties or fifties one is too old to start applying for a new job! Redundancy or retirement can be real sources of bereavement, especially if there is nothing very purposeful with which to fill the time. Work has been such an important part of life, especially if loyalty to one's employer has been a factor. But not any more! In situations of recession there is more competition and less opportunity out there, in the commercial world, so the position can become very pressing.

Three of us were sitting in the conservatory having coffee, reminiscing over old times and catching up on family news:

'And how is retirement going?' I enquire of him.

'Oh well, it still feels like a holiday because I haven't got into a proper routine yet. Though I hate the thought of getting old. I'm an action man and I like initiating things and I have great ideas about what I'd like to do now. And what do you think of this? I went to a lunch for retired professionals the other week and the speaker thanked us for all we have contributed to the community. "However," the speaker continued, "don't forget that we are planning for the future and there is an endless number of retired professionals like you in this area."'

'Wow!' I think.

'Imagine that,' says my friend. 'I have a fund of hard-won experience and wisdom and no-one wants it.'

After a minute or so, which added to his discomfiture I said, 'Yes, that's the first painful learning curve for you in this area. There are more to come!'

He couldn't believe his ears. This was a big and painful learning curve.

In an effort to jump to the rescue, his younger, extrovert wife said to me, 'Oh, you are such a pessimist! Life isn't really like that. You've got to give people something to hope for.'

I could only reply by asking feebly what this hope for the future was founded upon.

Is there any real difference between being a pessimist and a realist? Is a difficulty necessarily a disaster? How does one cope when it is?

The loss of a much loved spouse or friend often causes severe emotional anguish which seems to turn us into half a person for a time. John Donne the poet and one-time Dean of St. Paul's Cathedral wrote:

Any man's death diminishes me, because I am involved in Mankinde;[5]

---

[5] This is quoted in the book entitled: For Whom the Bell Tolls, a novel by Ernest Hemingway published in 1940. The title of the book, by Hemingway, and this quote is from John Donne's: Meditation No. 18 from Devotions upon Emergent Occasions, 1624. The novel is told through the thoughts and experiences of Robert Jordan, a character inspired by Hemingway's own experiences in the Spanish Civil War.

Nothing is ever quite the same again. The emotional pain involved in loss and separation by death is indescribable and—like old age—it has to be experienced to be understood. It is good to have new friends but the old ones who have known and shared our history are very precious and irreplaceable.

LEARNING CURVES: old age

We have eventually arrived at Old Age. What a journey! And the trouble is that old age creeps up on us gradually. One day we say, no longer in jest, I must be getting old. We begin to recognise that those changes which are beginning to occur are going to be permanent and this is a stage for which we have had no dress rehearsal.

The big difference between this last learning curve and the others which we have negotiated is that in this one we are not acquiring new skills or achieving some perceptible goal. We are having to unlearn much of what we have struggled to learn in our past life. There is just one skill left, however, and that is the most difficult and painful. We are trying to let go of many things and accept the new situation; to do it gracefully, without complaint, bitterness or criticism. Winston Churchill said:

> Let us reconcile ourselves to the mysterious rhythm of our destinies, such as they may be in this world of space and time.
> Let us treasure our joys but not bewail our sorrows.
> The glory of light cannot exist without its shadows.
> Life is a whole, and good and ill must be accepted together. The journey has been enjoyable and well worth making—once.[6]

All those learning curves, and the people who have helped, or not helped us, through them, have made us the person we are. T.S. Eliot said:

> Time past is time present.[7]

---

[6] This is a quote from what has become popularly known as: Let Us Be Contented, a poem from a collection entitled: Thoughts and Adventures (Amid These Storms), written in—or around—1932, by Winston Churchill. This poem has become a popular reading at funerals!

[7] This is a quotation from a set of four poems entitled: Four Quartets, by T. S. Eliot. that were published individually over a six-year period. The poems were printed them together in 1943 in America. They were first published as a series in Great Britain in 1944.

It is said that between the ages of sixty and seventy there is not much difference in the performance of a healthy mind and body. Between seventy and eighty there is a certain slowing down. Between eighty and ninety the slowing accelerates—and after ninety it is downhill all the way!

But the same big life-questions are: Where do I fit into society now? Who am I now? What of my future, if I have one? We have a past, but there is little or no future in this world (unless you believe in reincarnation).

Some four hundred years ago Shakespeare wittily, and truthfully, in the first four lines, summed it all up for us in Jacques' well-known speech in the play, As You Like It:

All the world's a stage
And all the men and women merely players.
They have their exits and their entrances:
And one man in his time plays many parts, his act being seven ages.
At first the infant,
Mewling and puking in his nurse's arms.
And then the whining schoolboy with his satchel
And shining morning face, creeping like snail unwillingly to school.
And then the lover, sighing like a furnace, with a woeful ballad
Made to his mistress's eyebrow.
Then a soldier full of strange oaths and bearded like the pard,
Jealous in honour, sudden and quick in quarrel, seeking the bubble reputation
Even in the cannon's mouth. And then the justice In fair round belly with good capon lined,
With eyes severe and beard of formal cut, full of wise saws and

moral instances,

And so he plays his part. The sixth stage shifts into the lean and slippered pantaloon,

With spectacles on nose and pouch on side, his youthful hose well saved, a world too wide

For his lean shank; and his big manly voice –

Turning again towards childish treble, pipes and whistles in his sound.

Last scene of all that ends this strange eventful history

In second childishness and mere oblivion.

Sans teeth, sans eyes, sans taste, sans everything.[8]

The first six stages of our lives seem so vital and important, but I have yet to hear anyone say that stage seven is fun or that they would like a repeat of it.

There is another account in the same vein, written by the romantic poet King Solomon in about 950 B.C.E. This is not so well-known. The words in italics and encased in brackets, is my own take upon these verses:

Remember your Creator in the days of your youth,

before the days of trouble come and the years approach when you will say,

'I find no pleasure in them' - before the sun and the light

---

[8] This is a quote from the play entitled: As You Like it, by William Shakespeare. This begins a monologue spoken by the melancholy Jaques. The speech compares the world to a stage, and life to a play. It catalogues the seven stages of a man's life—that are often referred to as the seven ages of man—and they are as follows: infant, schoolboy, lover, soldier, justice, pantaloon, and second childhood. The play is a comedy and it is thought ot have been written around 1599, and first published in 1623. The play is based upon the early romantic prose entitled: Rosalynde, by the playwright and novelist, Thomas Lodge.

and the moon and the stars grow dark, *(fading capacity for enjoyment)*

and the clouds return after the rain; *(increasing perplexity)*

when the keepers of the house tremble, *(legs)*

and the strong men stoop, *(spine)*

when the grinders cease because they are few, *(teeth)*

and those looking through the windows grow dim; *(eyes)*

when the doors to the street are closed *(ears)*

when men wake up at the sound of birds, *(sleep)*

but all their songs grow faint;

when men are afraid of heights *(lack of balance)*

and of dangers in the streets;

when the almond tree blossoms *(weakened sexual appetite)*

and the grasshopper drags himself along

and desire is no longer stirred.

Then man goes to his eternal home *(death)*

and mourners go about the streets,

Remember him - before the silver cord is severed, *(voice)*

or the golden bowl is broken; *(brain)*

before the pitcher is shattered at the spring, *(heart and general collapse.)*

or the wheel broken at the well,

and the dust returns to ground it came from,

and the spirit returns to God who gave it.

'Meaningless! Meaningless!' are the words of the Teacher.

'Everything is meaningless!'[9]

---

[9] From the book of Ecclesiastes, Chapter 12, verses 1 - 8.

Chilling, isn't it? Even worse than Shakespeare! But we can understand the expostulation at the end. What is the meaning of life? What is it all about? And why do we struggle through all these learning curves since we all end up in dust?

So what is all this about growing old gracefully? People talk a lot about it, but with all the negatives, success sometimes seems a bit elusive. What is the secret, if there is one, or maybe there is more than one secret? We shall try to explore this.

Obviously, this is not a new problem. The Bible, that was written so long ago by many different people at different times, makes reference to it frequently, and often encouragingly. There is one piece, that I have already quoted, which says:

> ...we finish our days with a moan. The length of our days is seventy years - or eighty, if we have the strength; yet their span is but trouble and sorrow, for they quickly pass, and we fly away.

The trouble is that nowadays, thanks to modem medicine, technological advances and certain social improvements, the length of our days even stretches to ninety or even more, at least in the Western world, if we have the strength. But do we really want to live that long? And for whose benefit?

It may seem like a good idea in some respects but people who are seriously old often think that enough is just about enough. Living too long can make problems for the next generation as well as for us. Are we any happier having the knowledge that we may live to a ripe old age, but that the end is inevitable and one day we shall fly away? Where shall we fly to? This is a prayer of strength and peace:

> Lord, support us all the day long of this troublous life until the

shadows lengthen and the evening comes and the busy world is hushed, the fever of life is over and our work is done. Then, Lord, grant us safe lodging, holy rest and peace at the last, through Jesus Christ our Saviour.

Amen.

Cardinal John Henry Newman

Remember your Creator in the days of your youth…
The length of our days is seventy years—or eighty, if we have
the strength; yet their span is but trouble and sorrow,
for they quickly pass, and we fly away.

Ecclesiastes 12:1 & Psalm 90:10

ATTITUDES

One very familiar response to the ageing process is an attempt to deny it. All of those advertisements for the cosmetics which are going to hide the wrinkles and restore our former youth don't always work out very well, do they? Also, what about the unpleasant description of someone who is mutton dressed up as lamb? We have to be a bit careful about what we wear and forget the fashion pressure. Occasionally we see a man who tries his hand at some energetic sport in an attempt to demonstrate that he can still do it. There is something rather sad about people who are obviously trying to hang on to the days of yore when they may have looked more attractive and seemed more capable. Denial is not a very satisfactory way of coping, really. It is too much like hard work because eventually the truth will out!

Another familiar way in which we try to make these unwanted facts more palatable is to joke about them. We all know about the aches and pains, the high blood pressure, cholesterol, osteoporosis, phlebitis, painful arthritis, difficult feet and all the other ailments which increase as time goes by.

We know about the anxieties, the unspoken fears, and the limitations that are so unfamiliar and unwelcome. But we laugh about memory loss, dentures that don't fit and hearing aids that don't work properly. By the way, why does everyone mumble these days, or talk so fast that they are almost unintelligible? Perhaps they do not realise that our ageing brains are not able to assimilate the individual sounds as quickly as they used to, and so this ends up in speech becoming just a muddled noise. There is no need for people to shout—they only need to speak more slowly and clearly and open their mouths properly! Many people do not realise that most people's hearing deteriorates with age, even if they are reluctant to admit it. Deafness is a major and serious handicap. It can lead to isolation and loneliness, not to mention the mutual frustration in attempting normal conversation.

You may have come across the typically flippant description of attitudes regarding old age:

>Kidnappers are not interested in you.
>
>In a hostage situation you are likely to be released first.
>
>People call at 9.00 a.m. and say: Did I wake you up?
>
>People no longer view you as a hypochondriac.
>
>There is nothing left to learn the hard way.
>
>Things you buy now won't wear out…
>
>You get into heated arguments about pension plans.
>
>You have a party and the neighbours don't even realise it.
>
>You no longer think of the speed limit as a challenge…
>
>Your eyes won't get much worse.
>
>Your investment in health insurance is gradually beginning to pay off.
>
>Your joints are more accurate meteorologists than the national weather forecast.
>
>Your secrets are safe with your friends because they won't remember them either.
>
>Your supply of brain cells is finally down to manageable size.
>
>Author Unknown

It is all very well to laugh at ourselves, perhaps it is one of the saving graces of being English! We might just shrug our shoulders and say, oh well, that's life! Or rather stubbornly, I don't care! Or, as my friend Irene said to me:

I don't want to go to hell, I shall know too many people there!

All of this laughing off does not really ring true, in the end. Actually, we do care, and we wish life were not like that, but we don't quite know how to handle it. We don't like the constant physical pain, the limitations and sometimes the enforced inactivity or aching loneliness which makes us keep the television on purely for company. While there are some funny aspects it is not, on the whole, a joy-ride and there are times when, if you didn't laugh, you might just cry. People react in different ways:

It's horrible; I hate it; I wish it would go away.

And lest she should give up altogether, Mary keeps her day absolutely full of commitments, of one sort or another, and then often complains that she never has any time! She finds her own company rather boring so she has to depend upon endless activity to keep her going.

And Bill, another friend, said to me, after a little thought:

The worst thing was when the car had to go. It felt like giving up my independence and it was extremely hard.

Bill's decision is truly difficult. It involves accepting a radically different lifestyle. He continues with:

Asking for lifts from other people can feel quite embarrassing although I know that there are plenty of people who would gladly help me.

We can understand what this feels like. Independence diminishing by the day.

But it is very much worse when we have to give up our home and all that it involves because we need more constant care. These huge adjustments are very painful to accept and they make us sort out our priorities rather ruthlessly. All of this can't be done in a hurry either.

There is another shock to the system for those of us who are busy doers and givers of help to all and sundry. We discover that we are more often on the receiving end of assistance now. This takes some getting used to, especially if we are the sort of person who needs to be needed. It takes a large degree of humility and graciousness to accept the fact that we are now the vulnerable and needy ones. However, in all honesty we have to admit that there are some crafty elderly souls who cash in on their helplessness as a subtle—and almost unconscious way of controlling other people—we have seen the sweet old lady, whose daughter is being driven to distraction by her mother's gentle and persistent demands. This has probably been a life-tong habit, but becomes more obvious with age. It can produce some unhappy emotional by-products of resentment!

I heard an interesting comment from an elderly lady who said:

When you are old you become a nonperson. When I am out with my daughter people usually talk to her and not to me, as though I were not there. If I happen to be sitting in my wheelchair, people talk to her, even if they are talking about me. This can be exasperating!

Some of us become aware that we old people tend to talk about ourselves all of the time, conversation tends to revolve around our ailments, our grandchildren or our pets. This is understandable when our physical limitations have narrowed considerably and our scope of life mainly confines us to our home.

One little old lady I know, Edna, is suffering from macular degeneration and a major degree of deafness, as well as arthritis and other conditions that are common to the elderly, but she keeps her apartment in an immaculate condition. I ask her:

> 'Why ever do you need to do all that dusting and cleaning everyday?'
> She replies: 'I do it to keep my personality. If I just sat around all day I should turn into a nothing and I don't want that.'
> She is ninety-three and she has huge difficulties in her daily life because of her problems, especially the lack of sight.
> 'God looks after me,' she contentedly comments.

There is not much that this lady can do all with her time, as she can no longer read, write, sew, go shopping, cook, watch television or do the things that she would have enjoyed previously. She is so grateful for the things she can do, like listening to endless tapes and the many aids which the Royal National Institute for the Blind can produce.

I have met another very happy, lively widow lady who is in her nineties. She lives alone and tells me that she forces herself to walk up the stairs rather than use her Stannah lift:

> ...even if it takes me half an hour. You've got to keep mobile while you can.

Though she is in her nineties, she still manages to go out to various day centres most days, and while she is waiting for her transport to arrive she sits on the bottom stair where she can see the traffic. She continues to tell me:

> ...and while I am there, sometimes for half an hour, I just pray for people.

These two people are making a valiant effort to cling on to the ever decreasing degree of independence that they still have. It is tremendously costly in regard to the level of effort that is required by them, but it is the remains of their previous determination and positive attitude to life, and their faith in God that keeps them going.

ATTITUDES: loss

One of the sad facts of life is that in old age we begin to lose dear friends and people whose history is so bound up with our own. One by one our contemporaries leave us and we wonder who will be next? Despite harbouring these thoughts that cross our minds from time to time, we have to persist and go soldiering on with our memories, knowing that our friends are missing. We feel the loss very keenly, and often for a long time. We feel diminished, part of us has become paralysed. Again, the Bible, that is so relevant and up to date, captures the sadness of our loss:

> As for man, his days are as grass; he flourishes as the flower of the field; the wind blows over it and it is gone; its place remembers it no more.[10]

There comes a time when we have to let our loved ones go. Sometimes it is a conscious decision to let them rest in peace, rather than to keep them in a memorial shrine of our own making.

Of course we have to remember that there are many younger people who are struggling with a diminished lifestyle and a similar deep sadness; we are not the only ones to suffer when bereaved. Those who are younger than us may have similar tough problems to our own, with reduced mobility, which foods to avoid, and all of those pills upon which we are so dependent. But those of us who are old do well to think about, and pray, that apposite prayer said to be the thoughts of an anonymous seventeenth century nun:

> Lord, thou knowest better than I know myself that I am growing older and some day will be old.
>
> Keep me from the fatal habit of thinking that I must say something

---

[10] From the book of Psalms, Chapter 103, verses 5 - 6.

on every subject and on every occasion.

Release me from the craving to straighten out somebody's affairs.

Make me thoughtful but not moody, helpful but not bossy.

With my vast store of wisdom, it seems a pity not to use it all, but Thou knowest, Lord, that I want a few friends at the end.

Keep my mind free from the recital of endless details, give me wings to get to the point.

Seal my lips upon my aches and pains. They are increasing and the love of rehearsing them is becoming sweeter as the years go by. I dare not ask for grace enough to enjoy the tales of others' pains, but help me to endure them with patience.

I dare not ask for improved memory but for a growing humility and a lessening (sic) cocksureness, for when my memory seems to clash with others.

Teach me the glorious lesson that occasionally I may be mistaken.

Keep me reasonably sweet, I do not want to be a saint—some of them are so hard to live with—but a sour old person is one of the crowning works of the devil.

Give me the ability to see good things in unexpected places, and talents in unexpected people.

And give me, Lord, the grace to tell them so.

Amen.

Surely this must contain some of the secrets of growing old gracefully!

ATTITUDES: time and rhythm

So how does it come about that growing old has, on the whole, such a bad press when it is an obvious and unavoidable process and everyone knows that it will inevitably involve limitations and probably some amount of pain? Certainly, it has something to do with time and the rhythm of life. One day rolls into the next quite relentlessly, and the older that we become, the faster time goes by. I used to hear my mother say this, and I thought it was rather silly, but I was young and quite naive, with limited life experience, but I still knew everything! This reminds me of the well-known quip, that is commonly attributed to Mark Twain:

> When I was fourteen my father was so ignorant I could barely stand to have him around. When I got to be twenty one, I was astonished to know how much he had learned in seven years.

The apparent increasing speed of the passage of time may have something to do with the fact that we are slowing down. Therefore, for some of us, the day has half gone before we have really got started.

The demise of some things, autumn for instance, brings the beautiful golden richness of maturity all of its own. It is sad, though, when the things, animals, or people, that we love begin to get misshapen and find themselves unable to function properly physically, and sometimes mentally, as they age.

It is particularly distressing to have to watch a loved one, who has been so responsible in previous days, gradually losing the thread of life. I read the following article by the journalist, Andrew Pierce:

> For me, one of the first signs of what was to come was not when Dad kept forgetting things, but the shock of hearing him deliver a four-letter tirade against Mum. Truthfully, at the age of 35, 1

had never heard him utter any profanity other than 'bloody'. He worked in a car factory where I presumed some of the blokes on the assembly line swore like troopers. If Dad joined in, the language stayed at British Leyland. And God help us kids if we ever raised our voice against Mum, let alone swear at her. But Dad who sprayed the air with expletives was not well. He was going through a phase of Alzheimer's. There were many others: when he became violent; when he told the people in shops that Mum had stolen his money—he would hand his wage packet to Mum every Thursday; and he had forgotten. It was tough, too, when he asked who I was. Repeatedly.

So was the first time I tied a bib around his neck to feed him. As was taking him to the toilet I'm not sure who cried most. Me probably. Despite the fact that his brain was degenerating, he still knew that grown-up sons don't do that for their parents. Which is why, ten years on, I can still feel the sensation as he clung to me, tears coursing down his cheeks, whispering into my ear, "I'm so sorry."[11]

Professor Ian Deary, Professor of Differential Psychology in Edinburgh University, asserts that:

>...understanding the ageing mind is one of the biggest challenges facing 21st century science.[12]

All of nature and life seems to work in a recurring rhythm including

---

[11] From the Daily Telegraph, 3rd March, 2007.

[12] Professor Dreary made this comment during an interview regarding: The Disconnected Mind Project. Details on this project can be found at:
http://www.disconnectedmind.org.uk/Home.aspx

within our own bodies—our heart beat, breathing, birth, death, etc... Both time and rhythm seem to be the music of life and the functions of this tune appears to be to work both creatively and destructively almost simultaneously.

Everything is on the move; all of creation is constantly changing and transforming; the mountains, the landmasses, and human life—nothing is static. Things always have to go and something else will take their place. In the end our first childhood turns into a second childhood, and we, ourselves, may need some assistance to cope with walking away from the people whom we taught to walk! History itself goes around in circles; empires come and go. And so, The World Wags.[13]

So called primitive peoples have used the rhythm of nature from time immemorial. Horological time is a relatively recent invention. Among all of this rapid circle of change, the only constant factors seem to be God and human nature! I wonder if it would be true to suggest that the elements of time and rhythm have only existed since the creation of the cosmos? What do you think? In the creation story in the Bible (which is not given as a detailed scientific account) we read that:

There was evening and there was morning - the first day.[14]

Although one day in terrestrial time is the same as a thousand years (i.e. an infinite time span) in the Creator's calculations—in other words, some state of affairs exists where there is no such thing as time—was time initiated for the benefit of living beings?

---

13 As well as being a quotation from Shakespeare's play: As You Like it; How The World Wags is a recording of Social Music for a 17th-century Englishman. This was originally recorded on 7th and 8th October, 1980. It was originally released by Hyperion Records on CDA66008. For more details please go to:
http://www.hyperion-records.co.uk/al.asp?al=CDH55013
14 From the book of Genesis, Chapter 1, verse 5.

It is almost impossible for a human mind to imagine eternity—a time when time has never existed, but just the other day I came across a very well known hymn. This seems to be trumpeted out on most state occasions in spite of its sepulchral tune:

> Before the hills in order stood,
> or earth received her frame,
> from everlasting thou art God:
> to endless years the same.[15]

That seems a fairly succinct description of a difficult concept. I read an amusing comment the other day:

> Cricket is a game, which the English, not being a spiritual people, have invented in order to give themselves same conception of eternity.(i.e. waiting ages for nothing to happen!).

There is a saying from the wise King Solomon, which he wrote in his observations on terrestrial time:

> There is a time for everything, and a season for every activity under heaven…a time to be born and a time to die…
> He (that is God) has also set eternity in the hearts of men; yet they cannot fathom what God has done from beginning to end.[16]

What does that mean? Could it imply that human beings do have some vague nation of the existence of a timeless state—maybe after death perhaps?

---

[15] Words: Isaac Watts (1674 - 1748), 1719. This is hymn can be sung to different tunes. The most commonly used tune is: St. Anne 1708, and the composition is attributed to William Croft, 1678 - 1727.

[16] From the book of Ecclesiastes, Chapter 3, extracts from verses, 1, 2 and 11.

ATTITUDES: inevitable changes

So there is nothing intrinsically wrong with old age in itself: it is just the fundamental rhythm of all life. It is our attitude to the inevitable changes that is important: acceptance is essential—resentment is very destructive. Obviously, a person's temperament affects the issue. The natural optimist may have a slightly less difficult journey up the steep learning curves of old age than the natural pessimist, but seldom is it an easy climb for anyone.

One of the characteristics of old age is that we find change of any sort something of an effort. We feel put out at the slightest thing, if someone sits in our usual chair, for example! Holidays can also be problematic. It is not that we don't like holidays, if we can manage them, but it is simply too much trouble to cope with all of that packing, the journeys and the upheaval. We are content to stay where we are, carrying out our safe routine and living in our familiar surroundings. We are not being lazy, ungrateful or stupid, it is just that we are getting old and that's how it is. Recently, a man came to my neighbour's door trying to persuade her to change to an allegedly much more advantageous electricity provider. She told him:

> My son-in-law will come round in an hour to sort things out with you. He understands all this, but I am old; I don't like change. I know where I am just now and it confuses me to have all this messing about.

Apart from my neighbour being fortunate in having a capable and willing son-in-law to call upon (a rare commodity indeed), the patience and the loving care of our friends and family is something that is very precious, and becomes evermore so as life progresses.

The young (I am referring to those in their sixties) are sometimes baffled by this. They are familiar with our being relatively intelligent and able to manage things ourselves, but they cannot fathom the condition of change. They, themselves, have never been old so how can they really understand, from the inside, what is going on and what it feels like? But we old ones can understand the attitude of the young because we have been there and done that. But not any more. We once had their energy. Sometimes we envy their vitality and acumen. Even a fairly healthy person in their seventies has no real understanding of what it is like to be in their nineties. They are not there yet and a great deal of difference has taken place in twenty years! Really old age has to be experienced to be understood.

In her gentle prize-winning novels describing old age, the American author, Marilynne Robinson depicts an aged retired minister whose explosive objections, on occasion, used to startle the church elders. As a consequence they began to draw their own conclusions about his mental state. Then, at home, he would say more than once, when the decorous turmoil of his soul happened to erupt at the dinner table with words like, 'As if I were a child!' This was a situation that his adult children had not foreseen. Neither had they realised that their father's body could become both a burden and an embarrassment to himself, and to them. The old man was certain that his problems inspired all sorts of condescensions, he became furious on the slightest pretext and he was anxious to demonstrate that he was still compos mentis.[17]

> ...therefore, we do not lose heart. Though outwardly we are wasting away, yet inwardly we are being renewed day by day.[18]

---

[17] I refer to the novels entitled: Gilead; and: Home, by Marilynne Robinson.
[18] From the book of 1 Corinthians, Chapter 4, verse 16.

God's constant message to his people is one of support and rescue:

> Listen to me, O house of Jacob,
>
> all you who remain of the house of Israel,
>
> you whom I have upheld since you were conceived,
>
> and have carried since your birth.
>
> Even to your old age and gray hairs I am he,
>
> I am he who will sustain you.
>
> I have made you and I will carry you;
>
> I will sustain you and I will rescue you.[19]

---

[19] From the book of Isaiah, Chapter 46, verses 3 - 4.

To whom will you compare me or count me equal?…
Remember the former things, those of long ago;
I am God, and there is no other;
I am God, and there is none like me.

Isaiah 46: 5 & 9

CONTRASTS

When I was at university (over half a century ago!), I remember our economics lecturer expounding the Malthus theory of population. It is one of the few things that I remember. Everyone knows, of course, that this theory states that population tends to increase faster than the means of subsistence and must therefore be controlled by methods which he suggests.

I remember the graphic illustrations of two triangles. The apex of the first triangle represented the proportion of elderly people in the country at that time, and the base represented the large number of people who were boosting the economy or pushing prams. It would have looked something like this:

I can't remember how the second triangle became inverted, but it was intended to represent the change to come in sixty years' time (which means now). The apex of this triangle would come to represent the wealth producers, we were told. The long base would represent the wealth-draining dependent aged who were being pushed along in their wheel chairs. This can be illustrated as follows:

At the time this all sounded totally implausible. However, sixty years later it has turned out to be an uncannily accurate forecast.

I understand that the United Nations designated the October 1st, in the year 2008 as: International Day for Older Persons! No special age was stipulated in this grand declaration, but it is clear that the fastest growing group of the older population, in the West, and certainly in this country, is those who are eighty years old or more. Simultaneously, with this edict of the UN, came the release from the UK Office of National Statistics showing that pensioners now outnumber teenagers by eleven and a half million! National attention is now being drawn to the plight of many elderly people who have hitherto been neglected, and to the geriatric problem generally.

One of the profitable private enterprises in this country now, is the provision of residential care for the elderly. This provision raises several rather big problems, not least the thorny political issue as to who foots the bill, the state or the individual. People have a real dread of ending up in one of the less imaginative care homes where the residents sit around the walls in armchairs in various states of somnification, waiting for the next meal-time. Although their physical needs are usually met adequately and there is kindness and patience on behalf of the staff, there is often little mental stimulation or any incentive to do anything. Visitors to these care homes often pick up a sense of pointlessness end depression. The more comfortable homes are often prohibitively expensive.

But as age creeps on, the energy and desire for something new and exciting wanes, sleep becomes more desirable with the security of knowing where we are and what is going to happen next. We feel safe in the environment that we know and are fairly content to stay there, however unenterprising it may seem to onlookers. Our bodies are wearing out and we feel less confident in our balance than we once were. All the same it is regretful to experience the deterioration of our faculties. Other people often notice that there is an accentuation of traits that have always been in our character, like an inability to make decisions, or a loss of self-confidence, obstinacy might increase, or a tendency to become depressed, are just a few examples.

Despite our diminished state and condition, one cannot feel that we still have something to offer, a purpose if you will. It is just that we get around to doing less, and when we do, it is at a slower pace, but our contribution is just as worthwhile, isn't it?

CONTRASTS: our physical apparatus

What an amazing thing our body has been, and still is! We have grown to know it well over the years and we become quite fond of it, in spite of its various creaks and groans. Consider this: it has its own central heating and ventilation systems; its own food storage compartments; different forms of recycling and waste disposal units; its own mini first-aid post; a pharmacy and in built alarm system; an exceedingly complicated computer which beats the most modern pieces of man made technology hands down, and this is protected by a carapace; there is a pump that works not stopping once for years on end, without which the entire complex would came to a full stop; and there is also a pair of bellows which keep the rhythm of the pump in working order. And there is so much more!

All of these systems are designed to work in harmony both independently and interdependently; they are all wrapped up in a waterproof elastic bag which allows liquid to came out but not come in. The texture of this bag varies according to its particular function, for instance the skin on the face is not the same as that on the sole of the foot—fortunately!

But even this is not all! This whole composition operates without any conscious control on our part; it just happens of its own accord. Once one of the systems has been put into operation it needs no interference from us. For example, when we have swallowed something it has gone out of our reach; the body just works its magic. Even when we are asleep the general bodily system goes on operating automatically. The dreams which seem inexplicable to our conscious mind may seem meaningless though they can be frightening; a miscellany of unconnected nonsense.

But some of the things in our experience are hidden away in our unconscious mind because for some reason we were unable to digest them emotionally at the time. Because of the potential emotional discomfort that may be involved, they can only be exposed in disguise and in the dark, appearing to be out of touch with conscious reality. It is fascinating to recall that our dreams are often embroidered with memories of people and places in our childhood. This serves as another reminder of the importance of those earliest years.

Neither is that all that this wonderful body has in store for us! That waterproof bag, the two little oscillating lights in the carapace, and indeed, almost every other part of the whole configuration, registers very accurately, in one way or another. If there is emotional distress or tension somewhere, the body and the emotions respond together accordingly. It is known that the eye is the window of the soul; our intestines and our skin also may react strongly to stress. Sometimes, though, a physical dysfunction can have an unrecognised emotional origin and this is usually labelled psychosomatic. Of course, any severe or painful physical disorder frequently effects the emotions and it is hard to endure a constant nagging, or a piercing pain or disability without beginning to feel frustrated or depressed.

In spite of this garbled, and somewhat brief, description of our anatomy, it is really wonderful that the entire organism functions so harmoniously, but not surprising that it begins to wear our after a while.

There is also something else. When we were younger our body was the vehicle which transported us from point A to point B. No longer! When we are older, our body tells us what it can or it is prepared to do. If we do not heed its supply of information then we pay the price.

At last, we are beginning to learn that our body has very accurate wisdom of all its own. It has always been so, but when we were younger we could ignore it more easily without serious results. It takes time for us to learn that our body does have its own accurate wisdom.

While you are contemplating all of this, perhaps in your bath (incidentally showers were not invented to promote contemplation), let us consider the well known words of another Psalm:

I praise you because I am fearfully and wonderfully made;

your works are wonderful, I know that full well.[20]

---

[20] From the book of Psalms, Chapter 139, verse 14.

CONTRASTS: the generation gap

There are many helpful things for those of us who are classed as the older generation. We are given senior citizen rail cards; free bus passes; disabled parking discs; a 10% discount when shopping on Wednesdays at B&Q; helpful gadgets in the house; free prescriptions; help with the cost of heating our homes when over sixty (even more for the over eighties); and all manner of other helpful things.

Also in the world of our social lives there are just a few advantages. You can sit down when you are tired at a party, while everyone else has to stand on their aching feet for hours on end. You can 'fall in love' with everyone and there's no harm done because there are no expectations on either side. You can also be just a bit rude, with a joking smile, and people will say with a retaliatory smile:

Oh, take no notice. She's losing her marbles.

Very occasionally, someone might possibly offer you their seat on a bus, which you must of course accept with an appreciative smile. It all reminds me of a poem by Jenny Joseph:

When I am an old woman I shall wear purple with a red hat that doesn't go and doesn't suit me.

I shall spend my money on brandy and summer gloves and satin sandals and say we have no money for butter.

I shall sit down on the pavement when I'm tired

And gobble up samples in shops and press alarm bells and run my stick along public railings...And make up for the sobriety of my youth...[21]

---

[21] This is from the poem entitled: Warning by Jenny Joseph, taken from: Philip Larkin's, Oxford Book of 20th Century English Verse.

Mind you, things are not what they were! The generation gap is getting wider. Young people seem to have such an appalling lack of manners. They put their feet on the furniture; they forget to say thank you; they drink from big thick mugs instead of the beautiful china which we used when we were younger (the delicate china teacups of a bygone age, seem to find their way into a variety of charity shops nowadays). The young also seem to have an innate problem in spelling correctly; neither can they do mental arithmetic—it is all gadgets and the like, such as mobile phones, games consoles and computers, all of these incorporate the latest technological wizardry. The following was said, by a panic stricken fifteen year old, whose mobile phone had just ceased to function:

> I can't get in touch with anyone; I'm completely isolated; I don't know what's going on; I can't speak to anybody.

What has happened to face to face communication? Even our ordinary language has changed. We now read about such things as blogs, blackberries, iPods and other such terms or words, some of which have apparently acquired a new meaning. Every day some new piece of incomprehensibility seems to have crept into our previously rich language such as, cu l8tr!

The list of new terminology and the gadgetry that accompanies it, is endless. But this is only one side of the story. There are, of course, plenty of the young who are courteous, unselfish, honest, loving, well motivated and doing enterprising things. What a relief that is! They are a pleasure to meet. It is very easy for us be thought of as grumpy old people, but we are not grumpy at all. It is just that society's values and attitudes are changing rapidly and we, the elderly, regret the loss of a more stable and less self-centred lifestyle. We do realise that some older people who have been in the habit of using computers etc, do find them invaluable for keeping in close touch with their families who live some distance away by e-mail, through web-cams, and by surfing the net. But usually, as one grows older one wants something simple. I just want to be able to switch if on or off; but now there are about a dozen different programmes that have to be negotiated to get anywhere and it all gets too complicated. It all presents too much of a challenge to a tired mind.

I saw an anonymous contribution in a local newspaper. It was a fun obituary. It read as follows:

Today we mourn the passing of a beloved old friend by name of Common Sense, who has been with us for many years. No-one knows for sure how old he was, since his birth records were lost long ago in bureaucratic red tape.

He will be remembered as having cultivated such valuable lessons as when to come in out of the rain, why the early bird catches the worm, and that life is not always fair.

Common Sense lived by sound financial principles (don't spend more than you earn) and reliable parenting strategies (adults, and not the kids, are in charge).

His health began to rapidly deteriorate when overbearing regulations were set in place.

Reports of a six-year old boy charged with sexual harassment for kissing a classmate; teenagers were suspended from school for using a mouthwash after lunch; a teacher fired for reprimanding an unruly student only worsened his condition.

It declined even further when schools were required to gain parental consent to administer aspirin to a student. However, they could not inform parents when a student became pregnant and wanted to have an abortion.

Common Sense lost the will to live as the Ten Commandments became contraband; churches became businesses and criminals received better treatment than their victims. Common Sense finally gave up the fight after a woman failed to realise that a steaming cup of coffee was hot, spilled a drop in her lap, and was awarded a huge settlement.

Common Sense was preceded in death by his parents, Truth And Trust; his wife Discretion; his daughter Responsibility and his son Reason.

He is survived by his four step-brothers, I Know My Rights; I Want My Rights; I Want It Now and I'm A Victim.

Not many attended his funeral because so few realised he was gone. If you still remember him, pass this on, if not, join the majority and do nothing.

In breaking news, we have just learned of the sudden passing of Common Sense's twin sister Common Courtesy, who died earlier today. We've also just learned that the well known criminal, It's All About Me, has been charged with criminal negligence in her death. Funeral arrangements have yet to be announced.[22]

---

[22] This is a modified version of an original article that is accredited to: Lori Bergman. You can learn more at: http://www.loriborgman.com This article, or poem, has been around the internet block an awful lot. Allegedly it was even used in an email to spread a virus, lol! Quite how this works is beyond my comprehension.

CONTRASTS: advantages

Despite everything, there is one huge advantage in being older for those who are fortunate enough to have grandchildren. What a tremendous amount of joy they can bring. The relationship between grandparents and the young can be very special. They can discuss things with their grandparents in a very different way from the way they would with their parents, and from a child's innocent eye-view Grandpa and Grandma has the time. It is such a privilege to cultivate such a close relationship where one has the joy, but not the total responsibility that comes with child rearing. There is also the added benefit that the children can sort out the mysteries of that wretched computer!

Grandchildren can be noisy and rumbustuous, it is such a pity that we cannot pass on to them all of our hard-won wisdom, they must discover it for themselves and we hope that such gems will not be gained by too hard a route. The accumulated experience and values that we can pass onto the younger generation is like gold dust and it will live in their hearts for years. Sometimes, in these modem days of so many working mothers (a strange phrase that—for it implies that mothers who stay at home to care for their children, full time, don't work), it is the grandparents who give much of their time and limited energy to the bringing up of children.

This is perhaps the greatest bonus of old age. It is that irreplaceable store of valuable experience and acquired wisdom. In Eastern countries old people are still respected and venerated, grey hairs are a sign of understanding about life, having been taught by it. Unfortunately, in the West, we have become obsessed with the youth culture. Children have to grow up so fast these days and they seem to be deprived of the care-free fun of exploring, pretending, discerning appropriate freedoms and the boundaries of life and how to make something out of nothing with just their imagination. What does this bode for the future?

Some time ago I asked a young relative of mine, Robert, to do a small piece of market research among his first-year university student friends on what they thought about old age. He, like many of his contemporaries is finding great fun in doing outrageous and crazy things. His first comment was:

> We are scared of old age in the sense that we do not want to endure all the perceived indignities.

Pictures of old people on the television, or possibly a visit to someone in a care home has produced this gloomy picture. Many expressed a dread and a fear that this could happen to them and that they would like to die in their sixties before they became too old. These students pitied old people because of the way that they perceived life had taken its toll. They thought that this fear is reflected in all of the many anti-aging, anti-wrinkle, plastic surgery and cosmetic advertisements. This led them to agree that the world (i.e. the West) has become a much more youth dominated place. One reason why elderly people are thought to know so little is that technology moves so fast and that they are getting left behind. Both Robert, and his friends, agreed that elderly people have a lot to offer, and he commented that:

> It is your elders that you learn from the most. I think of all that I've learned from you and Grandpa and Granny. So much of my moral understanding, beliefs, values and outlooks have been influenced by family. But, although there may be a lot of respect for family members, there can be a definite lack of respect for strangers, as illustrated by the fact that they are often targeted by muggers and con-men.

These observations led Robert to conclude that there are two elements in society which need support—the young and the elderly—and maybe sometimes the elderly do get overlooked. He added that on the whole his feedback was more than positive in his peers opinion, respect and appreciation for the older generation in our society. He went on to observe:

> I believe we owe so much to your generation and most of us feel guilty about destroying everything. In that respect we can see why the elderly, in turn, dislike my age bracket, because we are changing and have changed so many aspects of society.

There was an interesting article in the Sunday Times a few weeks ago, which it seemed to sum up the whole situation fairly neatly. It was about Immigrants and Natives and went something like this:

> People over forty are the Immigrants. We have come from a culture in which it was the norm to go to the library to do our research if we wanted to know something specific, then we would check the facts that we were told about, e.g. our car insurance. We would listen to what our teachers were saying and we would make notes for later use. If we needed to know the meaning of a word or how to spell it we would consult a dictionary. If we wanted to communicate with a distant friend we would find our notepaper and send a handwritten letter. One of our favourite pastimes was to curl up with a lovely book—preferably a hardback—and we would revel in the use of language and the descriptive elements which fired our imagination. People don't seem to do things the old-fashioned way any more. We live in a world of electronics and abbreviations and we feel marginalised and a bit isolated. It is

perhaps reassuring to know that the UN adopted Five Principles for Older Persons: i.e. independence, participation, care, self-fulfilment, dignity. (Resolution 46/91). Good idea, in theory!

On the other hand, if you are under 40 you are a Native who has been brought up in a culture where everything happens instantaneously and effortlessly—we hear of a first-class graduate who says he has never read a book. You want to go to Canada? Choose the location, e-mail to place your reservation, you get a confirmation almost immediately, you pay by credit card and the whole operation is concluded in half and hour with no hassle—all done by a click of a few buttons. You can find anything out on the internet without getting out of your chair or using a dictionary or an encyclopaedia and the general impression is that you can do anything, anywhere, at any time. Natives live by visual images in an instant society rather than by listening and thinking.

One wonders about the accuracy of some of the information; where does it come from and who put it there? Although the internet is neutral, why does it become so addictive and alarmingly prone to misuse?

You know when I sit down and when I rise up; you perceive my thoughts from afar;

You perceive my going out and my lying down.

You are familiar with all my ways…

Such knowledge is too wonderful for me, O Lord.[23]

---

[23] From the book of Psalms, Chapter 139, verses 1 - 4.

How precious to me are your thoughts, O God!
How vast is the sum of them!
Were I to count them,
they would outnumber the grains of sand.
When I awake,
I am still with you.

Psalm 139: 17-18

LETTING GO

Now we come to one of the last gradual slopes in our long journey of learning curves as old age finally catches up with us. Along this part of the climb we are actually going downhill which is usually more taxing than going up. There are jagged points which cause special difficulty and many smaller problems which are not so obvious to an observer. Letting go of things which matter to us is usually painful. Even throwing away worn out pair of slippers can fill us with regret for a few minutes. The new ones feel so unfamiliar and stiff and they take some time to know the shape of our feet. As we grow older the occasions for letting go seem to come more frequently and in bigger chunks. Hitherto we have been busy accumulating life's accessories as well as a good deal of experience and maturity. Now all that seems to become eclipsed by the needs of our body and, our failing memory and gradually increasing general frailty.

One particularly deep and jagged edge is the time then we have to let go of our home which is full of poignant memories and the results of our scrimping and saving, thinking and planning. We have to summon our courage and look the facts in the face. Am I going to be able to manage this house or would I be better in something smaller in a few years' time? I am already finding the garden more of a burden than a pleasure and I don't want to see it going to rack and ruin, that would just be too painful. How near am I to relatives or friends who might be able to give me some help if needed? What about public transport to shops, or to the surgery, hospital, or to wherever I need to be—and all the rest of the similar considerations? It is no good waiting until my family or the social services have to decide for me, and for them, what is the best. I must make my own decisions, face the regrets, and the pain and the grief that is involved while I am still able to think coherently about it and manage the upheaval of it all. That is a really sharp and painful jagged edge.

I see a local man in a local home for the elderly who is very bored, resentful and unhappy because he says that:

>...my family have dumped me here.

He is, in fact having much better physical care and comfort than he had in his own home, but he has found it too hard to make the break himself at the appropriate time. It is vital to give ourselves the time that is required to weigh up all of the practical pros and cons while we are sufficiently compos-mentis and physically able to cope with the upheaval of a move. On the other hand, I hear another man saying, quite demonstratively:

>I am demanding to stay in my own home until I die. It is so full of memories.

His family was being put under great strain, because they could not face the guilt of letting him down. It was a kind of folie à deux.[24] This mutual distress was understandable, but it blocked the way to any resolution of the problem

There is also the essential but unwelcome task of making a will. We actually have to face ourselves with our own death and what that involves. If we have not been able to galvanise ourselves to do it before, it now becomes extremely important.

---

[24] Folie à deux is from the French for: a madness shared by two. It is a rare psychiatric syndrome in which the symptoms of a delusional belief are transmitted from one individual to another. The same syndrome shared by more than two people may be called: folie à trois, folie à quatre, folie en famille or even folie à plusieurs (the madness of many).

LETTING GO: grief

Someone once said:

>Life seems to consist of one loss after another.

Sometimes it is the painful loss of a spouse or friends. It is not easy to make new friends and our physical and financial circumstances may hamper these efforts. In any case, new friends, lovely though they are, are not part of our history in a way our old familiar loved ones were. We can't share private jokes with new friends, or reminisce in the same way. Sadness and sorrow sometimes seem to be our main companions. If we have no-one to be at our side in public, we feel like half-a-person, almost deformed and certainly conspicuous because part of us has departed from our side. Where have they gone to? What are they doing now? Are they still aware of us in some way? Life seems so pointless if it just ends in death. But, as our life has to go on and as the years go by, we sometimes find our loved ones gradually receding from our emotional touch, though not from our memory, although we do not want this, it just seems to happen.

Grief-work often takes a long time before a new sort of equilibrium is achieved. We have to grieve fully and not push our feelings under the carpet where they will make their uneasy appearance later. Sedatives are not a good solution; they might help to relieve the pain but they do not resolve the grief.

After we receive the news of the death of a friend, or when we are given the diagnosis of a life-threatening illness, our first thoughts are often on a practical level and they surround our physical care, the welfare of the family, the management of our financial affairs, etc. It takes time for the painfulness of the situation to sink in and gradually be assimilated into our emotional life as well as our cerebral life.

With any major shock we feel emotionally numb for a while. It may take a few months before we realise that we may be sliding into depression, or that a few tears might come upon us quite unexpectedly from time to time. We are facing the biggest shock that we shall ever have—letting go of life itself as we know it.

This may be a time when we are grieving over all of the losses that have not been adequately mourned previously by us. We may be tempted to try to pull ourselves together but that is not the way. Although we may not fall apart altogether, we try not to carry our heart on our sleeve too publicly. But grief, with all its pain, must be experienced fully. It is always a lonely journey. People may grieve with us but no-one can grieve for us. It is a very personal process. It is something we have to do for ourselves but it does help if we can share our grieving with selected family or friends. They also may have some grieving to do as they share with us.

LETTING GO: regrets

As life moves onwards, one thing that we may need to face are our regrets. There are things that we have not done, and places we have not visited but it is too late when you are old. Maybe it does not matter much really. However, there may be things in our relationships with other people which need to be sorted out, now, before it's too late. There are misunderstandings which have lingered on and cooled our once warm friendships, or unresolved anger about something which still smoulders and mars our attitude to one another. Maybe we still have some unpleasant memories of which we have to let go: perhaps we have to be gracious enough to apologise, or receive an apology, so that we can leave with a clean slate and prepare for a *good death*.

For all of us it is hard to let go of the past with its special joys, sorrows and memories, even if we are not facing imminent death. We treasure them and life will never be quite the same again. We live in the present, not the past and we have to move on. It can be counter-productive to spend too much time in wistful reflection: I used to be able to... but now... or, when I was younger I used to... It is important to be glad about those things and thankful for what we can do now, rather than make negative comparisons. We shall never regain the strength and our vitality of previous years and we have to let them go. We have to draw a line under that chapter of youth and although it is still a part of our loved and very personal book, we don't go on reading it to ourselves or to other people over and over again. It is like making a conscious decision to move into the slow lane.

Of course people have different chapters in their lives and everyone handles them differently. There are many other tiny forms of letting go between the bigger ones. For instance the need to wear more sensible, and quite dreary shoes instead of the smart ones that we used to enjoy is a practical necessity! These are just pinpricks by comparison to other aspects of relinquishment, but they still hurt a bit, although we don't talk about them.

As time and events progress we may gradually find that our confidence is being eroded. Physically, our balance is not what it was and we live in constant fear of failing and have to go very carefully with our stick or walking frame of some sort. We can really do without the inconvenience of a broken leg or arm! We look at the travel brochures with their inviting pictures of far-flung places, but even going on a cruise now, with all of its convenience, may not be an option, for one reason or another. We just have to enjoy looking at the pictures in the glossy magazines and perhaps the distant memories that they may evoke. We become spectators rather than participants. Recently, I have been watching my friends play croquet—not the aggressive game that it is commonly thought to be— the proper game is more one of skill than brute force! Once, long ago, I was a champion but now I have to be a reluctant observer.

One huge problem is the deterioration in our sight. We take this precious gift so much for granted but gradually we need larger print, then a magnifying glass and then we have to let go some of our cherished hobbies. And so it goes on, as the scope of life becomes more limited.

Mentally, our memory also seems to lose track of things and we can't remember people's names, or the words which used to come so easily. Sometimes our financial affairs become all too complicated and we are grateful for the help of someone who is more astute, and perhaps most importantly, trustworthy.

The odd doze becomes a more frequent occurrence and it is quite easy to become preoccupied with our aches and pains; but it's a relief to just occasionally, be able to stop being cheerful and putting on a brave front. It is a relief when we can be honest for a few minutes and tell someone just how awful things can be at times. Rightly, it has been said that old age is not for sissies. I would concur with this simple statement, as bravery and fortitude is a prerequisite for ageing.

When we ourselves become old, we have to remember that unless other people have experienced illness or frailty they cannot fully understand, though they may be very sympathetic. They have not been there or done that.

Another thing that can be very hard for some of us to give up is our compulsive need to be in control. It comes so naturally to want to get everything organised and straightened out, but we have to learn to keep quiet on many occasions and we have to wait for others to take the initiative. This is not always so easy when we have felt responsible for so long; but now we are not the ones who are in charge any more. We have to leave it to others without helping, which is often interpreted as interference! They may not do things our way, but no doubt they will manage! We have to stand back and be patient, growing old gracefully and not bossily!

Increasingly we become dependent upon the availability of others to help us and perhaps make decisions for us. Our younger friends and family have their own busy lives to lead and instead of our being able to visit them when we feel like it, we now have to await their convenience. It is sometimes hard not to feel a bit neglected and ignored when intervals between the visits seem to get longer and we know that they are enjoying a busy social life elsewhere. But how lovely it is when they do come and visit us, quite spontaneously!

All of this letting go adds up to the gradual loss of our independence as we grow seriously older. That is the often the hardest thing for some of us to accept.

There is another little problem which some of us have made for ourselves. It is about whether we are just being lazy and letting other people do things for us because we can't be bothered with them ourselves? Could we be exerting ourselves more or are we genuinely lacking in energy? Or, perhaps we like living on the never principle, i.e. never stand when you can sit; never do today something which you can put off till tomorrow; never do something yourself which you can leave to someone else. Good idea, if you can find people who will cooperate!

Another strange thing is that, in a way, we live in two worlds:

Ellen, a younger woman, was working herself into a minor frazzle because the wallpaper was not an exact match with the curtains. There was such an outburst of anger and disappointment!

I was thinking Oh Ellen, does it matter to that extent? You can't take them with you, and when you are in heaven you won't be too bothered about matching wallpaper.

Of course, I am old and I have one foot firmly in heaven and the life after death already, so my perspective is different; I have to remember that Ellen lives in another perspective and that matching wallpaper is very important to her at this moment. In this way, I have to live in both my worlds.

LETTING GO: replacement

The big question is, if we let things go what do we put in their place? Although our part usually consists in watching other people achieving things, we can make a significant contribution ourselves. In Western society, for many years, a person's value has been calculated on how much they can produce or achieve. Does this mean, then, that when our achieving days are more or less over, we are of no value? The late Bishop of Winchester, John V. Taylor, has written that:

The oldest delusion of all time is that life consists of achievement.[25]

Could this be one reason old people are often neglected by society and their families? It could seem like that, if there is no-one left who loves us.

I am writing this in nature's season of mists and mellow fruitfulness. The leaves are decked in glorious colours, reds, yellows, browns and gold. But they are falling all around making little piles on the grass. Autumn is letting go the joys of the summer and these leaves will make compost for next year's growth. There are empty spaces where old plants been pulled out and they will remain vacant until next year. Hanging onto the old does not give enough space for the new to develop in due course. Letting go is trusting that one season will follow another as the creation pattern was intended. Could we let go of some of our clutter and extraneous involvements which hide the opportunities for fresh insights and new contributions? That may involve leaving some areas of our lives feeling a bit empty for a while.

---

[25] From the book entitled: Matters of Life and Death, John Vernon Taylor, 1914 - 2001.

LETTING GO: awareness

What significant contributions can we make? Old age offers us the tremendous gift of time and more quietness. We can be available; we can offer a listening ear, watch lovingly, and fill in the gaps, sometimes. We can think, encourage, pray and support in a dozen ways, and be there for other people. There may be times, when it would be appropriate, for us to warn about of the proximity of some potential rocks of which the young are too busy to be aware. Done sensitively and with known love, this can be immensely important in the life of some younger person, but we have to earn the right to speak, and we may not always be listened to!

In this frenetic world there are so few people who are prepared to be aware, available and free from the need to be doing something useful. It is so much more important to be, rather than to do; to be content to live within our own skin and thus have resources to give to other people, rather than gathering most of our resources from outside ourselves. Old age can mean that we have accumulated plenty of inner resources which our younger friends may not have not yet achieved—perhaps some of them are the blackberry-pluckers.[26] As we grow seriously older we develop a different perspective on life. Our values change and our mobility is more restricted. We may find ourselves pondering such things as What is life all about? What are the things that really matter and will last? Perhaps we have been too busy living. Someone once described this as:

> …the worries of this life, the seductiveness of money and the desire for other things…

There comes a time when we need to turn our attention to more abstract and spiritual matters.

---

[26] A phrase from the poem by Elizabeth Browning. Please see footnote 42 on the following page.

Our older years could be our first real opportunity to expand our own living and awareness. The difference between someone who is physically living and someone who is physically dead, is in their quality of responsiveness. A living person will move if touched and they are aware of what is going on around them. But there are people who are so occupied with the routines of their daily lives—such as the shopping, general chatter, television, arranging the next piece of entertainment etc—that any activity, however trivial, keeps boredom away because that can lead to depression and loneliness. They do not really want to get too involved in other people's lives and it is easier to ignore the little vibes which we all give off. Such people seem to have become unresponsive and virtually dead to the great transcendence all around us. They may seem relatively untouched by some intense music, and the profound beauty and order of nature does not seem to speak to their heart in enjoyment that is beyond words! Even the wordless depths of grief may seem to pass them by to some extent. Elizabeth Browning expresses this much more elegantly in her poem Aurora Leigh:

> Earth's crammed with heaven
>
> And every common bush aflame with God; But only those who
> sees takes off his shoes. The rest sit around and pluck blackberries
> And daub their faces, unaware;
>
> More and more from its first similitude.[27]

We have all met people who are kind, but we do not seem able to register very accurately what we are trying to express to them, neither do they

---

[27] From the poem entitled: Aurora Leigh, by Elizabeth Barrett Browning, 1806 - 1861. This poem was first published in 1857, at the height of Browning's literary career. The poem is one of the longest poems in English literature, encompassing 11,000 lines of blank verse. It traces the life and the artistic growth of a female poet, Aurora Leigh.

make much of an effort to understand us. We feel a bit empty after our encounter with them. They are the people who are not really aware, or deeply responsive.

Many people live in the rational and material world, unaware of the big world of the supernatural and the transcendent. T. S. Eliot describes them as:

> Living and partly living;[28]

Bishop John V. Taylor also says that for a long time he has been under the conviction that God is not hugely concerned as to whether we are religious or not:

> What matters to God, and matters supremely, is whether we are alive or not. If your religion inhibits your capacity for life or makes you run away from it, you may be sure God is against it, just as Jesus was.[29]

I find that these are stimulating thoughts!

In old age, we have the precious gift of more time, can we use it to cultivate a deeper awareness and responsiveness to the bigger world outside of our little personal one? This depth only comes when we can stay with personal silence and stillness. It may be that within our internal stillness we are doing some easy knitting or quietly playing with the dog, or some other undemanding thing at the same time, leaving our mind and body free and receptive for new thoughts and attitudes. For some

---

[28] From the verse drama entitled: Murder in the Cathedral, by T.S. Eliot, 1888 - 1965. This verse drama portrays the assassination of Archbishop Thomas Becket in Canterbury Cathedral in 1170. It was first performed in 1935. T.S. Eliot drew heavily upon the writing of Edward Grim, a clerk who was an eyewitness to the murder.

[29] From the book entitled: Matters of Life and Death, John Vernon Taylor, 1914 - 2001.

of us it may be that such quietness represents a threat that is too difficult to hold onto: it is sometimes too demanding to get involved with other people and their deep, hidden feelings, or even to be aware that God may have something to say to us. Perhaps we have been so busy "doing" all of our lives and it is too late to change. Nevertheless, if we can learn to use some of our time in quietness, we are making an invaluable contribution to other people's lives, and to our own, although it has to be measured on a different scale.

Night-time can be a dark and lonely place, especially in the small hours when we are at our most vulnerable. Everything crowds in on us and it can all be rather frightening, but, mercifully, all of these lettings-go do not happen together, usually, it is a gradual process and as we progress along the path we get a little more accustomed to the ups and downs. During this particularly hard learning curve our spirit is sustained by the experiences of the compassionate love God has for us and our trust that He will not fail on any of his promises:

A man's life does not consist in the abundance of his possessions.[30]

Fear not. When you pass through the waters, I will be with you; when you walk through the fire you will not be burned. For I am the Lord your God, and I love you.[31]

---

[30] From the gospel of Luke, Chapter 12, verse 15.
[31] From the book of Isaiah, Chapter 43, verses 2 - 4.

So do not fear, for I am with you;
do not be dismayed, for I am your God.
I will strengthen you and help you;
I will uphold you with my righteous right hand.

Isaiah 41: 10

WAITING

We all know about waiting, we do it every day and the older we grow, the more of it we seem to do. Hospitals seem to offer the best places to practise the art of being patient, when we are in the Out-Patient department or in the ward.

We wait anxiously for the doctor to come to us and reveal the result of that recent important test. We are told that he will be here in about an hour or so, and so we wait. An hour later there is no sign of his imminent arrival. Two and a half hours later he comes rushing in full of apologies. He has been very busy, of course, but I am exhausted with trying not to be impatient.

I have begun to realise why hospital users are aptly called patients!

A few months ago I had to have a bronchoscopy in order to find out what was going wrong in my lung. This procedure involves the insertion of a very narrow tube through the nose. At the end of the tube is a tiny camera and some rather sharp apparatus that can be employed for extracting a small piece of relevant tissue. In order to make all of this painless and less uncomfortable, the nose and throat are anaesthetised. I was glad to know that there was no need for fasting overnight, but for eight hours before the actual operation time there was to be no liquid intake of any sort.

In my case the procedure seemed to go according to plan, and did not take very long. The doctor and nurses were chatting among themselves so I assumed that they were not worried about anything, but it is not a procedure that I would wish to repeat, though there are far worse things about!

When it was all over with I was put onto a recuperation bed and left to cough and sleep. I asked if I may have a cup of tea, I was so very thirsty after hours of dryness. My request was met with a firm refusal by the nurse, with:

'Oh no, your throat is still anaesthetised and you might choke. You have to wait for two hours.' The nurse might as well have said two weeks.

'I can't possibly wait that long. I don't mind if I do choke but I need tea,' I said.

The nurse grinned and said, 'Sorry,' and she just walked off leaving me to watch the hands of the clock crawling round, much more slowly than usual.

Those next two hours were worse than the whole of the previous hour. I tried to sleep and think; I tried to remember poetry, to count backwards—anything to take my mind off that awful thirst. At the end of an hour and a half, I was wriggling and fidgeting and losing patience with myself. But lo and behold! Five minutes before the end of my torture, my nurse appeared with a real cup of tea—the best I have ever had in my life and a most delicious tuna and mayonnaise sandwich. I could have kissed her!

Now that life has calmed down again, I ask myself, why was I so irrationally agitated by having to wait? I knew that I was in safe and in benevolent hands—I certainly wasn't in some concentration camp or in a torture chamber—and I knew the hospital staff would be aware of my needs. I also knew that the time would eventually pass and that fretting was not going to speed thing up, so why could I not just wait quietly? Maybe there was some chemical urgency and perhaps I thought that I was halfway to dehydration, but, with hindsight, a clue came to me. I am so used to being able to meet my own needs and able to organise my own comfort that being helpless and dependent was an unfamiliar situation and against my natural emotional grain.

Perhaps I have given a rather extreme example with all sorts of extenuating circumstances. A more everyday example would be when I was having difficulty in getting in touch with someone on the phone. I was becoming slightly irritated because there was no reply, when there should have been. As I waited, I reflected and began to realise that below the bottom line of all of the excuses was the fact that the situation was beyond my control. I was left feeling helpless and frustrated. This is never a comfortable state to be in!

Then came a day when I was waiting for a bus. It arrived twenty minutes later, but sitting in the sun had been quite pleasant although the wind was a bit strong. Sometimes this bus does not come at all and I was beginning to wonder whether this was one of those days. But it did not matter much. My shopping was not urgent and could be done another day. I wondered to myself, what made the difference between waiting for a cup of tea in a hospital ward, a phone call and a bus? I realised that I was in control of the bus situation—not of the bus itself of course—and of my own reactions to its lateness, I could have gone home and done the shopping another day and that made the difference between waiting, with all its frustration, and being able to wait patiently. I am reminded of the old Serenity Prayer:

> God, grant me the serenity to accept the things I cannot change;
>
> Courage to change the things I can,
>
> And the wisdom to know the difference.[32]

Does our instant society contribute to the generalised need to take the

---

[32] This prayer is most commonly attributed to being written for a sermon by Reinhold Niebuhr, perhaps as early as 1934. The prayer is cited by Niebuhr in his book: The Essential Reinhold Niebuhr: Selected Essays and Addresses, and by Niebuhr's daughter, Elisabeth Sifton, in her book: The Serenity Prayer: Faith and Politics in Times of Peace and War. In the past, the prayer has been adopted by Alcoholics Anonymous and other twelve-step support programs.

waiting out of wanting and thus making waiting and trusting an alien and very unfamiliar experience? Our plastic cards in our wallets has come to mean that we can have whatever we want, whenever we want it, regardless of our ability to repay the debt with interest. This has been one of the factors which has led us into a national problem of very severe economic proportions, not to mention the slide into national immaturity.

We all vary in temperament and some of us are more laid back than others. Some of us seem to be fundamentally anxious, I can't help it we exclaim; I am made like it. I suppose it all depends upon our genes and early life experiences. When we are waiting, and we are not in control of the situation, we have to place our trust in someone or something else, and that is often the reason for our impatience. Trust is so difficult, especially if we are unsure of the reliability of the person or the thing we are trying to trust. Lady Luck is not the most reliable person either! Perhaps you know the tale of a child who, when asked to define faith (which is the same as trust), replied that it is:

Trying to believe in something which you know is not true!

A lot reflects our experiences of waiting when we were very young. Most children want instant gratification. They might say, I can't wait; I want it now! But, as we grow up a bit and we experience promises that are honoured, and when boundaries are kept, because of consistent love which can say no, as well as yes, it becomes a little easier to wait with less immediacy. How fortunate we were if we had good and loving parents— but none of us had perfect parents—such people do not exist! However; they (like God) make good whipping boys. It is tempting to blame other people for our failures, but when we are adult we are accountable for ourselves.

The emotional stress of waiting in important circumstances often seems to override the rest of life which has to manage somehow an autopilot, for instance, when we are awaiting an unconfirmed diagnosis or a job application.

In life there are other significant times of waiting when there are no agendas and no fixed deadlines, such as retirement, unemployment or being struck by some major and long term disability. Previously we were in control of our own lives, and maybe other people's, but now we are tempted to feel redundant and unvalued while everyone else seems to be doing something worthwhile.

People who have not learned how to wait can be difficult friends, spouses or colleagues.

WAITING: waiting patiently

There is a big difference between just waiting and being able to wait patiently. The latter displays an important aspect of our life—growth into maturity. Learning how to wait is one way of developing character; it trains us in patience, self-control and trust and it enables us to wait, not without concern, but without undue worry and stress. Waiting is seldom comfortable but *one of the secrets of growing old gracefully is the ability to wait patiently.* The inability to wait patiently and the predisposition to worry, are similar to the two sides of the same coin.

The inability to wait patiently depends largely upon what we are doing while we wait. So what could we be doing, when just waiting? How are we to deal with the uncomfortable tension during waiting periods? Here we are faced with the strength or weakness of our inner reserves and on what they are based. How strong is our trusting capacity and also, in what is that trust placed?

A specially problematic waiting time is the occasion of the elusive answer to our urgent prayers. One man experienced the agony of watching his thirty seven year old son die from a malignant brain tumour. He implored God, with all of the sincerity he could muster to heal him, at least for the sake of the children. What happened? His son died. This leads to the inevitable raft of questions, such as, where is God? It is so unfair! Why, why God, why? The sight of seeing our offspring die before us has a special pain. In his anguish and bitterness the father cried out:

> What's the good of prayer? It is a waste of time. Just what sort of God allows this sort of cruelty to happen?

At that point he closed his heart to God and in his uncomprehending anger slammed the door and hid deep in his heart a hard ball of anger.

We are with this man in his intense pain which still shows itself years later. The ways of God are indeed mysterious and in our frustrated attempts to understand, we often reduce God to our own size. But if we are able to hang in there, rather than banging the shutters dawn on the pain, anger and confusion, there is the possibility of growth into deeper maturity of a spiritual sort and a strange ability to live with acceptance of confusion and mystery. This is experienced as peace.

We might know what Freud said about our need to create God as a substitute father figure for ourselves. If Freud were alive today he might well be more than a little surprised to discover that people have endowed his postulations with such authority. After all, he was only one of the early explorers of hitherto largely unchartered territory and he was breaking new ground which others have since modified, amplified or challenged. But there is help in some of the things that Freud said. However, the living God is not a sort of celestial Father Christmas who is there to give us everything we would like, or supply things that we think we need. Real love is sometimes tough and may appear, at first sight, to be negative. The love of God is the same. *Trust, or faith, is the only currency which we can use when we have to do business with God.* If there were no such thing as doubt there would be no such thing as faith.

Sometimes faith is hard for us, even though we may have had some real experiences of God's faithfulness in the past. Trust in his love— even when it seems tough—and the assurance that *He* is in ultimate control because of his kept promises and due to our previous experiences, become an even more important factor in our life as vulnerability and dependency increase in advancing years. Trust (or faith) enables us to wait more patiently and it contributes, in no small measure, to our ability to grow old a bit more gracefully. We are not always waiting in faith to get our own way and have what we want, we are simply putting the control of things into the hands of the living God and what a relief that is! He has his own way of doing things, so we have here one reason why waiting patiently is so difficult for some of us. Without realising it we have become control freaks and our need to be in control is yet another of those things of which we have to let go.

As we grow old, we gradually become aware that we need more help with the exhausting little jobs involved in daily living and thus, having to accept the vulnerability, dependence and waiting that is involved. We have to await the convenience of other people. We know that there are people who would be glad to help, but we don't like to ask. It is sometimes hard to find the balance between being a nuisance and being appropriately needy. And what about professional carers? The need for a carer seems to be confirmation of an unwelcome loss of independence.

The following poems, sayings and verses mean a lot to me. (I keep a little book with favourite sayings that I have come across):

Lord, what a change within us one short hour
Spent in Thy presence will avail to make—
What heavy burdens from our bosom take,
What parched grounds refresh as with a shower!
We kneel, and all around us seems to lower;
We rise, and all, the distant and the near,
Stands forth in sunny outline, brave and clear,
We kneel, how weak; we rise, how full of power!
Why, therefore, should we do ourselves this wrong,
Or others, that we are not always strong;
That we are overborne with care,
That we should ever weak or heartless be,

Anxious or troubled, when with us is prayer,

And joy and strength and courage are with Thee?[33]

If you can wait, and not be tired by waiting, you'll be a man, my son![34]

I waited patiently for the Lord;

he turned unto me and heard my cry.

He lifted me out of the slimy pit,

out of the mud and mire;

He set my feet on a rock and gave me a firm place to stand.[35]

The Lord is good to those who trust in him and the one who seeks him; it is good to wait patiently for the salvation of the Lord.[36]

In the morning, O Lord, I lay my requests before you

And wait in expectation.[37]

The Psalms were written out of first hand experience, in a world where violence oppression and arbitrary, motiveless tragedy caused people to challenge constantly and to doubt received orthodox wisdom: in other words in a world remarkably like our own.[38]

---

[33] Archbishop Richard Chenevix Trench 1807 - 1886, an Anglican Archbishop and poet. This full poem has been set to the Welsh hymn tune Ffigysbren.

[34] From the poem entitled: If, by Rudyard Kipling 1865 - 1936, a British author and poet.

[35] From the Book of Psalms, Chapter 40, verse 1.

[36] From the Book of Lamentations, Chapter 3, verse 26. This was said by Jeremiah who described himself as: having seen affliction and having walked in darkness.

[37] From the Book of Psalms, Chapter 5, verse 3.

[38] Gordon Mursell was Ordained in 1974. This is an extract from his book entitled: Out of the Deep.

But those who wait on the Lord shall renew their strength;
they shall mount up with wings like eagles,
they shall run and not be weary,
they shall walk and not faint.

Isaiah 40: 31

RESTING

While we are waiting we are often resting; just doing nothing in particular. Waiting is not just a waste of time! At long last, after a long life full of activity, we have the precious gift of *time*. But we are not very well versed in how to use spare time which may have come upon us unexpectedly because of our increasing physical fragility. What can we do with it?

One of the many things we can do is to spend longer time in prayer. What is prayer? Many books have been written about it and there are many different forms of prayer. We could start by saying what prayer is not. The most obvious thing is that, unless we have some knowledge of whom we are addressing, it is fairly pointless and seems more like superstition. The sudden request for a shorter queue can hardly count as a quality prayer: it is just trying to use God to suit my purposes. However, God is so gracious that He takes note of what is in our heart and that is the main factor. Our prayer does not have to be a recital of well rehearsed words or something that sounds impressive. We may be a novice at this sort of thing, but that does not matter at all.

We sometimes make arrow prayers, quick, short and sharp sentences in an emergency. Othertimes we present our shopping list to God composed of all the things that we would like him to do for us, or for other people. I suppose that this is alright in a way, but it does not make for a very close personal relationship, which is what prayer is.

The whole sum of prayer is that it is a two-way communication between someone who loves us, and a person whom we love. The style of personal prayer is really immaterial, although it is at times helpful to makes use of some of the beautiful, formal prayers written long ago. We have the immense privilege of praying for other people who are struggling with life's problems, for our friends and family, or for an array of different subjects. And, of course, we talk about our own situation though there is no need to explain it in detail to the God who already knows all about it. It is more a case of affirming our trust in Him and being ready to accept his will in loving confidence. Again I recall:

> And what a change within us one short hour spent in Thy presence will prevail to make…

There is a story about Mother Theresa: it may be apocryphal, I don't know. The story goes that she was being asked about prayer, her questioner asked of her:

> 'How do you talk to God?'
>
> 'I don't. I listen to him,' was the reply.
>
> 'What does he say to you?' came the next question.
>
> 'Nothing. He just listens.'
>
> 'What do you mean? I don't understand,' said the bemused questioner. To which Mother Theresa replied, 'If you don't understand, I can't explain it to you!'

Now, we are not all Mother Theresas and this may sound rather like a typical feminine response to an apparent conundrum, but it is not really so difficult. How would you explain the colour blue to a blind person? Perhaps you have to know or experience it before it makes much sense.

But this is the sort of delight that can await us when we have more time to wait and rest. A similar sort of experience is perhaps that of two lovers just enjoying each other's company, sometimes in silence, as just being together is sufficient. No words need be uttered, for they would spoil the moment. And the better that we know the person then the deeper becomes the listening. What if we feel too ill or tired to be able to do this? Our Lover knows what is in our heart and He knows what to do to restore some sort of peace or send a comforting visitor.

But we can only be waiting patiently when both our mind and our body are fairly relaxed.

We may be sitting quietly but we know that internally we are all fidgety and anxious to be doing something. Many of us who are natural doers and organisers of things feel more comfortable in that mode. But when we come to real rest of spirit, it involves letting go of this insatiable desire to be active. It is often useful to have paper to hand so that we can make a note of anything urgent, which needs attention—better than getting up at once to sort it out. Time and rest are two of the great gifts of old age!

RESTING: inner stillness

Why do we find it so difficult to be still internally? Is it perhaps because we have never had an opportunity to experience the richness of inner silence and apparent inactivity? Or maybe we have not yet discovered that silence and waiting need not be just a waste of time.

Sometimes it is hard not to feel guilty, because we are *not doing anything* when a situation occurs which seems to be asking for control and action. Actually we could be doing something, different from visible activity. Silence does not mean lack of any stimulus, mental or even emotional activity. The well known phrase of be still and know that I am God, implies plenty of activity! It is difficult to achieve this while our minds are obsessed with the cares of this world, however legitimate they might be. A great deal depends on which god we have set our minds to know, be it sport, money, music, celebrity culture, technology, cars or whatever.

Obviously, there are emergencies when we can't just sit around piously; but it is possible to be physically active and resting internally simultaneously because *we know the One who is in control.* Other religions and cults have their meditation routines, but we are looking towards *the Living God who is powerful and present* and who will not reveal himself until we are prepared to make room for him to speak to us.

For those of us who are troubled because our usual recourse to prayer or the Bible seems to have dried up; we may want to pray but it all seems like a fog. So what can we do? We just rest and wait, knowing that whatever it feels like, we are truly loved and letting go of our own struggles. We allow ourselves to be carried along in God's strong, loving arms. Experience of dryness may be known to many believing Christians from time to time, but any feeling of inaccessibility will pass. We just have to hang on in there.

Resting and inner stillness involves some effort, discipline and time. A great deal also depends upon our determination to value that precious commodity of time. When we are older we do usually have more time, or at least more choices in how we use the time we have.

In some ways, however, the general idea of resting seems quite appealing. Effort over, time for a break, a bit of peace and quiet, relief for those aching or tired limbs. Take sleep, for example, at the end of the day we climb into bed and relax. Ah, bliss! The jobs are done, people have been seen, problems have hopefully been solved. Now we can settle down to our little read, and arrange ourselves as comfortably as we can, around our various aches and pains, no more having to make an effort for a little while. Then, in due course, hopefully, we drift off quietly into no man's land. Our wonderful body will wake us up of its own accord when it is time for the comfort stop. All too soon the hours have passed and a new day has dawned, but bed is still the best place in which to be! The only thing wrong with sleep is that we can't enjoy it while we are actually doing it.

However, if precious sleep evades us, the night turns into our least favourite time. Hours of restless tossing can leave us exhausted and exasperated. Periods of rest or sleep are essential ingredients in the nature of all living things, human, animal, and vegetable. Physical pain or an unquiet mind might be the cause of our insomnia?

RESTING: two types of rest

Physical resting comes at intervals. We can't be doing it all the time. Rest is just a special little respite now and again for us to value. That is one good aspect. But there is another type of resting. We may know someone who always seems to be serene and at peace within themselves; any struggling that they may have to do is done quietly and in private. They do not seem to need to be the centre of attention or noisy in any way although they are taking a full part in life. These are the people who are learning about internal resting all the time; they have made at the centre of their lives a permanent space for quiet stillness and otherness. It is sometimes called transcendence, which the dictionary defines as going beyond normal physical experience.

As an example of this physicality, the image of a boat comes into my mind, it is floating quietly and peacefully on the water, a slight wind blows up and the boat rocks to and fro—but the anchor and the ropes are firmly grounded so the boat does not break loose or get washed away. We cannot expect to maintain a completely even keel throughout life at all times, and in all circumstances; sometimes we are attacked by fear, doubt, uncertainty, or darkness but our ability to remain still, inside ourselves, and restful in our inner hearts, relies upon our anchor and the rope and not upon the boat itself.

RESTING: what it takes

So how can we seriously get to grips with learning to be still and rest, as we grow older if we want to? Gone are the days for rushing about and packing activity into every moment; we have neither the strength nor the inclination for that sort of life now. The familiar phrases such as, it's too much trouble; or, I just can't be bothered; seem to be on our lips fairly frequently. Sometimes it seems as though we have lost both the energy and the will to exert ourselves to anything. Perhaps we should examine the way that we live. Obviously, there are the ordinary, daily things which have to be done, but sometimes it is easier to find something— anything—to do rather than make time to just sit and be still and silent. We might be familiar with the W.H. Davies' lines

> What is this life, if full of care,
> We have no time to stand and stare.[39]

As I have observed, standing and staring requires some discipline and concentration! Stillness opens up a different world of being, that cannot easily find entrance into our busy lives. Allowing time for stray thoughts to come to us; permitting realisations to dawn; becoming aware of the vibrancy of sounds and colours that we had not registered before, like the songs and habits of the birds; being able to appreciate things which we had never noticed, for example, the way lovely little flowers grow in the most unlikely places; all of the beauty and intricacies of nature all of which is far too profound for words, which George Herbert describes in

---

[39] These famous lines are from the poem: Leisure, by William Henry Davies, 1871 - 1940. The poet, Davies spent a significant part of his life as a tramp or vagabond in the United States and the United Kingdom. Eventually he became one of the most popular poets of his time. The principal themes in his work are the wonders of nature; observations about life's hardships; his own life as a tramp and the characters that he met.

his magnificent poem on prayer:

> …heaven in ordinarie…something understood.[40]

There are many great songs, and much prose, that espouses in words of praise the richness that comes from this sort of inner stillness, and from our being receptive to a glimpse of the world of heaven about us. Some lines from the poet William Wordsworth are very familiar such words:

> The world is too much with us; late and soon,
>
> Getting and spending, we lay waste our powers
>
> We have given our hearts away.
>
> A sordid boon!
>
> The sea that bears her bosom to the moon,
>
> The winds that will be howling at all hours,
>
> All are up gathered now, as sleeping flowers.
>
> For this, for everything, we are out of tune;
>
> it moves us not.[41]

People sometimes say that they simply can't find the time. Actually, we do not have to look for time; it is not drifting about like some lost item, nor is it hiding away. We have to make time by not doing some other thing. (The destructiveness and creativity of nature!) That is where the difficulty comes in. It is often more comfortable to be busy! Often we have to discipline our bodies to sit still and our minds to relax.

---

[40] This is from the poem entitled: Prayer, by George Herbert. This is often cited as one of the most profound depictions of prayer. It was published in 1633.

[41] This is an extract from the sonnet entitled: The World Is Too Much with Us, by the English Romantic poet William Wordsworth, and through the words he criticises the world for being absorbed in materialism. He sees a world that has distanced itself from nature. This sonnet was composed circa 1802, and it was first published in: Poems, In Two Volumes, in 1807.

RESTING: problems—frogs and lizards

Sometimes we come across people who are trying to ignore a previous part of their life because it was so painful—it may be an acrimonious parting, such as divorce, or an unhappy childhood, or something that has left an ugly scar. They think that these things are best forgotten, but these scars will not go away, because they are a real part of life just as much as the happy times. Submerged feelings of remorse, fear, resentment, ungrieved sorrow or some other disquieting emotion are often niggling away inside of us. If those painful times have never been fully faced and embraced they can never be really laid to rest. The memories may still remain as a fact of life, but the sting will have been drawn out when we can face those troublesome, painful and destructive issues. Sometimes we cannot do this because of lack of our own courage, or perhaps through the lack of a person, whom we trust enough to help us through. These seriously cancerous poisons, which may seem as though they have been buried away safely, will raise their insidious heads from time to time in negative attitudes such as withdrawal, depression, manipulation, over-compensation or excessive behaviour e.g. alcoholism, sexual addiction or self-harm. They may even take many different forms of physical symptoms such as constant headaches, back pain, etc... They are like the iceberg whose most dangerous part is out of sight underneath the water.

In order to achieve real rest within our inner spirit we have to look at both the good and the bad experiences or our life and acknowledge that they are truly ours, whether we like it or not. We can't split the painful bits off and still remain emotionally whole and healthy. When we can integrate these bad parts there comes a time when a comforting forgiveness and, perhaps, a better understanding and maturity, can begin to replace the bitter memories.

One of the Brothers Grimm fairy tales, The Frog Prince, is about a beautiful princess who could not find a suitable husband despite a desperate search. She came across a frog and he told her that if she would kiss him then she would find her husband. What? That slimy, ugly, repulsive thing! But she managed to do it eventually, and lo and behold, it turned into the handsome prince and they lived happily ever after!

The meaning of that apocryphal fable is obvious! There is a vivid and more realistic story of this sort of embracing that has to be done if we want freedom. In his book, The Great Divorce, the author C.S. Lewis describes a man who carried a destructive red lizard on his shoulder. It was constantly whispering negative messages to him about his grievances and lustful thoughts. The big angel offered to tear the lizard off and kill it. The man's agony of ambivalence in giving his decisive consent is believable and the screams of pain during the process. Secret obsessions can be very possessive. But the end of the red lizard cannot take place without the man's own clear consent. Freedom and peace come at a price.

We would all like inner restfulness and stillness of heart. We do not want our final years to be clouded with unpleasant memories and distressful thoughts. But the sort of true rest that we would like does not just fall out of the sky. It takes a considerable amount of single-minded strength of purpose to kiss our own personal frogs, or to part with our own red lizards. We sometimes need skilful, professional hands to hold onto us while we do so, especially when the problem is deep.

RESTING: an offer

We also read that Jesus said to us:

> Come unto me, all you who are weary and burdened, and I will give you rest.[42]

Those of us who have had a personal encounter with the very alive Jesus Christ know that this wonderful invitation holds real truth. We cannot prove it by anything except by our own experience and the witness of millions of people, who over generations have also proved this to be a life-changing encounter.

For some it has been a bit spectacular and its involved a painful struggle. For most it is a quiet assurance that there has been a fundamental and permanent change. This is where forgiveness can be found; the grace to deal with the hard things that spoil our lives, and the strength to cope with the vicissitudes of daily living. What a relief to be able to exchange our burdens for his rest! That is the good news of Christianity.[43]

But there is another clause which goes:

> Take my yoke upon you and learn from me, for I am gentle and humble in heart, and you will find rest for your souls.[44]

The promise is not just one-sided. It involves a commitment on our part. By submitting ourselves to his gentle discipline we discover that he does not inflict upon us sores which would chafe and harm us like an ill-fitting harness. His purpose is to give us life and help us to be more alive and aware, although we may not always understand what he is doing when the way seems strange and unfamiliar. This type of rest is an open

---

[42] From the gospel of Matthew, Chapter 11, verse 38.

[43] Please see the gospel of Matthew, Chapter 11, verses 28 - 29.

[44] From the gospel of Matthew, Chapter 11, verse 29.

invitation which we can receive or reject. Perhaps it is all summed up in these beautiful words (with its play on the word, rest):

> When God at first made man,
> Having a glasse of blessings standing by;
> Let us (said he) poure on him all we can:
> Let the worlds riches, which dispersed lie,
> Contract into a span.
> So strength first made a way;
> Then beautie flow'd, then wisdome, honour, pleasure:
> When almost all was out, God made a stay,
> Perceiving that alone of all his treasure
> Rest in the bottome lay.
> For if I should (said he)
> Bestow this jewell also on my creature,
> He would adore my gifts in stead of me,
> And rest in Nature, not the God of Nature:
> So both should losers be.
> Yet let him keep the rest,
> But keep them with repining restlesnesse:
> Let him be rich and wearie, that at least,
> If goodnesse leade him not, yet wearinesse
> May tosse him to my breast.[45]

And:

> In returning and rest you shall be saved; your strength lies in quietness and trust.[46]

---

[45] From: The Temple, by George Herbert.
[46] From the book of Isaiah, Chapter 30, verse 15.

DEATH—THE END OF THE BEGINNING

Now we have arrived at the end of our long journey up and down the learning curves. I have hesitated before writing this conclusion, because I have not yet been there, or done that. I'm sure that most of us would agree with Woody Allen's sentiment that:

> I am not afraid of death; I just don't want to be there when it happens.[47]

We would all like to die quietly in the night and bypass the pain, indignity and distress that the process of dying involves for some people. We are grateful that so much can be done these days to relieve pain and make the journey into the unknown less terrifying.

Archbishop Rowan Williams was right when he said in a recent Easter sermon, that in England we have grown so accustomed to a relatively luxurious lifestyle that we no longer know how to handle death. After the death of his father the poet Dylan Thomas wrote his famous words:

> Do not go gently into that good night,
>
> Old age should burn and rage at close of day,
>
> Rage, rage against the dying of the fight.[48]

This passionate outburst against the apparent hopelessness of death rings true for so many. Death has also been described as the enigma of non-being. This is not an exciting prospect! Perhaps that is why people are so

---

[47] Woody Allen (was born Allen Stewart Konigsberg; December 1, 1935) is an American born filmmaker, screenwriter, actor, comedian, jazz musician, author and playwright.

[48] From the poem of no title by Dylan Thomas, 1914 - 1953. This is a villanelle that was composed in 1951. It is generally considered to be among the finest works by the Welsh poet. It was originally published in the journal entitled: Botteghe Oscure, in 1952. It also appeared as part of the collection entitled: In Country Sleep. This was written for his dying father, and it is one of Dylan Thomas' most-quoted works.

reluctant to think about death. Healthy, active people in their seventies are still busy thinking about life, family, hobbies etc... and they make an almost conscious effort to dismiss the inevitable future apart from some of the practical arrangements which need to be made. Death has also been called: Sister Death[49] by St. Francis of Assisi—but she is an unpredictable visitor. Often when we long for her to come to bring release and comfort she seems to be either indifferent or too busy helping someone else. At other times she comes shockingly and stunningly uninvited.

> Because 1 could not stop for death
> He kindly stopped for me.
> The carriage held but just ourselves
> And immortality.[50]

---

[49] From the work entitled: Canticle of the Sun, St. Francis of Assisi, 1181/1182 - 1226. On his deathbed, it is reported that St. Francis recited, several times, the last addition to his Canticle of the Sun, the words: Be praised, O Lord, for our Sister Death. He also spoke out Psalm 141.

[50] From the poem entitled: Because I could not stop for Death, by Emily Dickinson, 1830-1886. Emily Dickinson was a prolific writer of poems, but fewer than a dozen of nearly eighteen hundred poems were published during her lifetime. Her poems are unique for the era in which she wrote. They are mainly short lines, they typically lack titles, and often deploy quite unconventional capitalisation, punctuation and general grammer. Many of her poems deal with themes of death and immortality. This is a poem that was composed privately, during her lifetime, but it was published after her death in 1886.

DEATH—THE END OF THE BEGINNING: immortality

We know about death, but immortality is an unknown mystery and we tend to feel slightly uncomfortable with things we cannot understand. We can plant our heads firmly in the sand and refuse to think about it, or alternativly, we can just deny its existence, or say that no-one has ever come back to tell us about it. *Wrong! Someone did come back!* But what stays with us, unanswered, is the constant question of just what happens after death?

It is so sad when we attend a friend's funeral and say our last farewells. We do not know what has become of them. They were lovely, but they have now faded into oblivion. Do we just go home and hope for the best and attempt to comfort ourselves by saying that after a long illness they are now at peace, or that they are in a better place? Perhaps we are consoled by reminiscing that they lived a good life and they are now at rest? But how do we know? In five years time who, apart from their close associates, will remember them and their life's experiences. The words of the Bible seem so horribly true as we think about some of our friends and look at their empty places:

> As for man, his days are as grass, he flourishes like a flower of the field. The wind blows over it and it is gone and the place remembers it no more.[51]

Perhaps we find it easier to read George Eliot's eulogy on Dorothea, Middlemarch's heroine, in which she describes the effect on those who lived around her to be incalculably diffuse like that of many who have lived faithfully a hidden life and rest in unvisited tombs.

The poor suffering and tormented Hamlet soliloquises upon the

---

[51] From the book of Psalms, Chapter 103, verse 15.

grimness of death in Act 3 Scene 1:

> Who would fardels bear,
>
> To grunt and sweat under a weary life,
>
> But that the dread of something after death,
>
> The undiscovere'd country, from whose bourn
>
> No traveller returns, puzzles the will,
>
> And makes us rather bear those ills we have
>
> Than fly to others that we know not of?[52]

---

[52] From the play entitled: The Tragedy of Hamlet, Prince of Denmark; or more commonly Hamlet, a tragedy by the playwright, William Shakespeare, 1564 - 1616. This play is believed to have been written between 1599 and 1601. The play, is set in Denmark, and recounts how Prince Hamlet exacts revenge on his uncle Claudius for murdering the old King Hamlet, Claudius's own brother and Prince Hamlet's father. The play charts the course of real and feigned madness—that includes overwhelming grief to incandescent rage—and the play explores the themes of treachery, revenge, incest, and moral corruption.

DEATH—THE END OF THE BEGINNING: the last enemy

We are told, in the Bible, that:

> The last enemy to be destroyed is death. For he "has put everything under his feet."[53]

The fact that death is 'The last enemy', is not difficult to believe. But we know that the heart of our Christian faith is that God has rescued us from the dominion of darkness by his own death and his subsequent supernatural resurrection. His resurrection is one of the best attested facts in history, being well documented in secular writings and also witnessed by many of the people who watched his horrific death. There were hundreds who saw him after his resurrection when he was a recognisable person who could eat and talk with them, and maintain the previous relationships he had had with them, although now he was in a different form. He had entered into the darkest recesses of the kingdom of evil and death and returned the Conqueror, never to die again. To quote the metaphor of a recent broadcaster (I cannot recall who said this) on BBC radio 4 on 18th May 2009:

> Jesus Christ was like a great diver who plunged into the depths of a hidden, stinking, murky swamp in order to rescue a priceless diamond. He resurfaced holding it aloft in triumph.

That resurrection was a seismic explosion of cosmic proportions which related not only to individual human beings but to the whole of the created universe.

With repeated familiarity, now-a-days we associate Easter celebrations with holidays, chocolate eggs and bunnies and we tend to forget the

---

[53] From the book of 1 Corinthians, Chapter 15, verses 26 - 27.

monumental impact of his actual resurrection but:

> ...this [grace] has now been revealed through the appearing of our Saviour, Christ Jesus, who has destroyed death and brought life and immortality to life through the gospel.' Here we have an authoritative definition of immortality![54]

I realise that not everyone finds it easy to believe, or understand this. Talk about death—let alone immortality—has become a taboo subject in our time, even though death is the only certainty we can have about our life: and it is perhaps the most important subject for us to consider. People have various thoughts about it. Hindus believe that we go through a continuous cycle of reincarnations until at last we arrive at perfection; some say that they hope that their Granny is looking down on them, from up there; some believe that their idol is really still alive and hiding somewhere (such as Elvis Presley). Others say that they live on in people's memories.

It is impossible and unproductive to argue with people about these matters of faith: one can only know that this belief is worthy of trust when one has proved the trustworthiness of the God who made the statement.

---

[54] From the book of 2 Timothy, Chapter 1, verse 10.

DEATH—THE END OF THE BEGINNING: heaven

We have various descriptions of heaven and hell through the poets and artists of previous ages. How can something that is unknowable to the human experience be so described? These accounts all seem to range from the boring, through to the gruesome, but it is from these accounts and from certain Biblical passages these impressions must have been gained.

For a start, we could ask: just where is heaven? The answer; we simply don't know. There is no justification for assuming that it is a physical place above and beyond the bright blue sky somewhere. It is more like a state of heart. For instance, when we are in an ideal situation, preferably with someone we love, it feels like perfection, and we might say, this is heaven! We say this, even though it may be a short-lived experience. One of the clues we have about heaven is the verse which says:

> No eye has seen, no ear has heard, no mind has conceived what God has prepared for those who love him.[55]

In heaven, probably the measurements of time and space have ceased to matter.

If this remarkably beautiful, but imperfect world is a sample of what awaits us, we can be sure that the next will be perfection and permanent; the reign of evil will finally be over and there will be no more sorrow, pain, war, injustice, destruction or death, which are evil's trademark.

---

[55] From the book of 1 Corinthians, Chapter 2, verse 9.

DEATH—THE END OF THE BEGINNING: faith

People do say to me, it's alright for you, you look so well and you have such a strong faith. If only they knew! I am grateful that I do look well most of the time, but it is not about the size of my often feeble faith, it is about the power that lies within that little piece of insignificant shell, called faith, which is the size of a tiny mustard seed. You can't get much smaller than that! It is also about the daily proven reliability of the person in whom my trust is based; otherwise it would be wishful thinking.

But when you think about it, the whole of life is about exercising faith. We get on the train and entrust our life to the driver whom we have never seen before and do not know anything about. Without thinking, we just trust that he knows what he is doing and is capable of doing it, but when it comes to trusting God, that seems to be a different issue. Why? After all, we could all learn to be train drivers if we wanted to, but God is in a totally different league! God is all mystery, unfathomable and way beyond the comprehension of the human mind. But, he also came as the living God and as such he experienced physical, emotional and spiritual suffering to an extent that we shall never experience. None of the gods of this world is a god of suffering and self sacrifice like this. Why?

We human beings like to be able to understand, control, and change things. It is uncomfortable and challenging to be confronted with mystery. Generally speaking, to the scientific mind, unless something can be analysed and proven it cannot be accepted without hesitation. Seeing is believing. Science is always researching, trying to push out the boundaries in an attempt to understand, uncover and then control things that were previously hidden and mysterious. We are often grateful and amazed at the things that scientific research has revealed and unearthed to mankind, although sometimes the scientists themselves are accused of playing God. Life is thought to be easier if it can be controlled and documented. It is even easier to accept an illness if it has a specific name by which we can handle it.

But faith works in a very different currency, that is distinct from controlling and being in charge. Faith is the ability to accept and the humility to submit. This is a totally different mind set! Faith is the only currency which God uses and it is mostly in evidence when the supernatural meets the natural; for instance, when our cry for help or mercy is greeted by his resources or a special kind of peace. The track record of God's faithfulness to his promises since the world began is impressive. Nevertheless, there are times when we do doubt and ask hard questions, but faith and genuine doubt are not in opposition to each other, as we have seen. They can often inform each other or cast us back onto some sort of faith. It is often a case of 'LORD, I believe; help thou my unbelief'. We may never have the answer to our hard questions. We have to be ready to live with uncertainty and mystery. This is not easy but it is God's territory. If we knew all of the answers we should be gods in our own right.

Of course, no-one was ever argued into faith, although it is important for us to ask questions and have enough intellectual satisfaction. Faith is sometimes like climbing a hill. At the foot, you have to decide whether this is a hill that is worth the effort or not. Books have recommended it, friends have waxed eloquent about it, but only when you, having committed yourself to the climb, do you begin to see brief glimpses of the surrounding landscape. Eventually, when you reach the summit, you see the stunning views that were impossible to see and comprehend at the bottom which other people who have been there have experienced. It was worth all the effort!

Talking of books reminds me of an interesting comment that I read in Barack Obama's book entitled: The Audacity of Hope.[56] He comments that several years ago, when he was teaching constitutional law at the University of Chicago, the professors of theology worked in lecture rooms opposite his and Obama often suspected that both he and they had similar problems with their students, in that the students felt that they knew the scriptures and constitutional law, respectively, without having really read and grasped the true meaning of either. They would use unrelated passages to support their arguments and they tended to ignore those with which they disagreed.

One does find that this happens a lot when people discuss matters of faith.

---

[56] The full title of this book is: The Audacity of Hope - Thoughts on reclaiming the American dream. It was published in 2007.

DEATH—THE END OF THE BEGINNING: decision time

My visit to my oncologist earlier in the day had left me speechless. He had said that the cancer had now spread to my liver. That was a surprise! I had had no indication that things were any worse than they had been for a while, but we all know what a spread to the liver means. I am now lying on my bed in the dark, wide awake, trying to take all this on board and wrestling with the decision which I must make within the next two weeks because there is no time to waste. I am feeling very isolated and bewildered. I can hardly believe that this is my body he is talking about. Previously I had faced this eighteen months ago when I was told that I had an inoperable secondary focus on my right lung. After the short, palliative session of radiotherapy I had recovered so well that I had begun to forget that cancer is not a benevolent friend; but this time it seems so final and imminent—possibly five months are left. We all know, in theory, that one day we shall die but that usually refers to other people.

I am fortunate in having good friends who will advise and support me, because I am a newcomer on this pathway to death and I need their help, but they cannot make the decision for me. They can only observe that everyone reacts differently. I have to decide between intravenous chemotherapy, as a trial, under the hospital's watchful eye, and to risk the usual unpleasant after-effects in order to live for a few more months with the unguaranteed possibility of a better standard of life; or I can opt for no treatment and let nature take its course with this body which has so many things wrong with it already. Many people have had to face this dilemma, but that does not help me now. Both pathways have their risks and problems and no-one can tell me which would be easier.

Suddenly the perspective on everything seems to have changed. What will the process of dying be like? Will I become emaciated? What shall I say to the family? What sort of care will be needed? Will it be available? The planned holiday does not seem to matter any more. Shall I be able to go to my niece's wedding in August? I shall probably never see little Emma Louise going to school. What is the unimaginable actually like? Questions galore to which there seems to be no answer. On this journey into the unknown I am alone with a multitude of mixed emotions, all in a big jumble and face to face with the prospect of death. I have already let go of many things, and now I am to face the final, ultimate, letting go of life itself.

I do not know how I shall be able to say goodbye to my loved ones. The sadness of the separation is unbearable. (I wonder if the pain of separation is the reason why people are so reluctant to talk about and face death.) But then I think of what and who awaits me on the other side, that makes the whole situation calmer—even quietly restful and peaceful. I can entrust my dear ones to the Lord for now, knowing that those of them who belong to the Christian family will join me one day.

DEATH—THE END OF THE BEGINNING: visitors

I am very fortunate in having so many kind friends who bring their love in all of the different ways in which they express themselves. Some come bursting in with good advice, reassurance, smiles and encouragement, chattering away nineteen to the dozen. If I have a chance to express my own feelings on the matter, I am sometimes given a little ditty about the visitor's mother-in-law (unknown to me) who was in exactly the same position as me and they coped extremely well. I am not terribly interested in the mother-in-law but I try to listen patiently, getting more and more tired. She is not in exactly my position, anyway. Eventually the clock comes to my rescue!

Then there are people who phone because they want to express their concern but they are unable to make a personal visit for one reason or another. They cannot see the facial expressions, or the effort to restrain tears; but those who phone in love, rather than out of curiosity, are usually sensitive to these things. In any case, a phone call is better than nothing even if it tends to keep things on a fairly superficial level. It is often a help if people who would like to come in person do make a short call to ensure that it would not be at rest or treatment time.

I hesitate to say this, but there are a few lovely Christian people who bring some helpful book, or verses from the Bible, which have been a comfort to them in their times of distress. (They may not have noticed a pile of books lying around my room, as yet unread.) Their Christian faith seems so sure that any element of doubt or pain appears to be beyond their comprehension. They may be extolling the virtues of the next world and praising the Lord with great enthusiasm. I too am praising the Lord, but more quietly and with more pauses in between. I am not quite sure of the next world yet, and am having to wait patiently to discover what it is all about, but I am certain that it must be too wonderful even to try to imagine. But the genuine desire of these kind people to help is very heart-warming and a comfort in itself although what they say may not be quite appropriate to where I am at the moment.

The person whose visit is most welcome is the one who can sit back and just listen. There is no need to talk. All I want is for them to be there, quietly empathising with my mood of the moment if they can. It should not be too hard; it is usually fairly obvious! These are the aware people. Listeners of this quality are few and far between. It is so much easier to talk. Silence is not always easy to hold; but it has so much to say in its own profound way. Questions do not always need to be answered and reassurances are sometimes just a desperate effort to stave off the painful and unanswerable questions. I do not want advice or explanations: the experts are there for that. Just being there, with me, is so important. Of course, I want to hear about what they are doing, their plans and to share our funny stories. I don't want the conversation to be focused on me all the time; sometimes I get very bored with thinking about myself, and besides my world has become rather small since I have become more incapacitated. Although so much of my attention is now on the next world, I am still very aware that we are all living in this one for the time being.

When we are old and ill we grow tired of struggling with our body which is slowing down and wearing out. This does not mean, necessarily, that we want to die. On the whole life has been both interesting and varied—sometimes good and sometimes hard—but we are just too tired and it feels as if it is time to go. It seems like arriving at the last chapter of a good book when there is an appropriate end. We would like to die a good death; a heart at peace with everyone; a body sufficiently sedated, if necessary, and to be comfortable enough to let go. If we have confidence about where we are going to it makes all the difference. Some sweet old soul once said:

> When I meet Jesus I shall say, 'Oh, I recognise you. We have been together for a long time.' And he may not be the only one we recognise!

DEATH—THE END OF THE BEGINNING: finally

What else is there to say? I decided to have no treatment so I am now in a strange waiting period which feels like no-man's-land. I sometimes feel a bit sad to think of parting with this old body which I have got to know so well over many years and which has been a good servant. Now it is more of a master, and I overstep the boundaries with unpleasant results. I am letting go of more and more of this world's goods and chattels and trying not to spoil today by imagining too much about tomorrow. As I let things go, I am thinking; 'Well, I can't take this with me, and I remember that the only thing we ever take with us into the next world is the precious personal relationship that we now have with the LORD.'

Am I imagining all of this, just deceiving myself in order to make the pain less? There are still so many unanswered questions and why is life so unfair? Or, perhaps:

> I have been half in love with easeful Death,
>
> Call'd him soft names in many a mused rhyme,
>
> To take into the air my quiet breath;
>
> Now more than ever seems it rich to die,
>
> To cease upon the midnight with no pain...[57]

I cannot imagine what heaven is like as I haven't been there or done that

---

[57] From the poem entitled: Ode to a Nightingale, by John Keats, 1795 - 1821. This play is believed to have been written between 1599 and 1601. John Keats was born in London, and became an English lyric poet, the archetype of the Romantic writer. Many of his poems show that he held a fascination with a world of death and decay. This poem was written in May 1819. It was composed in just one day. It became one of his odes and it was first published in a collection of works entitled: Annals of the Fine Arts the July of the following year. In this poem the nightingale that is described within the poem experiences a type of death but it does not actually die. Instead, the songbird is capable of living through its own song. Humans cannot expect to live on. The poem concludes with a reluctant acceptance that pleasure cannot last and that death is an inevitable part of life.

yet, and I am sorry I shall not be able to come back and tell you about it. I am prepared to take the guaranteed risk of trusting (faith) God's eventual and apparent conquest over the powers of evil and death, I can share in the sure and certain hope of the resurrection. So it is with deep gratitude that I can say that I am an Easter person!

Recently I came across an interpretation of what life after death might be like. I found it quite helpful, so decided to paraphrase it here. The Rev. Dr. John Stott says, when quoting C.S. Lewis:

> Christ's conquest of death also indicates the nature of his resurrection…We do not believe that our bodies will be miraculously reconstituted out of identical material particles of which they are made at present. Jesus himself said after his resurrection: "…a ghost does not have flesh and blood as you see I have" (Luke 24:39). But He also said that He would now be alive for ever and ever (Rev 1:18). Thus it would appear that he was raised from death and simultaneously changed into a new vehicle for his personality. The scars were still visible and people recognised his voice, but at the same time he could pass through a sealed tomb and locked doors.
>
> In a similar way, there is a combination between seeds and flowers. Seeds are plain little things but they will in due course present fragrant and colourful flowers.
>
> So we who are followers of Jesus, believers, are not looking forward to resuscitation (raised but not changed) or survival (a spirit but not a body). We are looking forward to a resurrection in which we shall be raised and changed simultaneously.
>
> The body that is sown is perishable, it is raised imperishable; it is sown a natural body, it is raised a spiritual body. For further reading see 1 Corinthians 15: 12 - 58.[58]

Therefore we do not lose heart...So we fix our eyes not on what is seen, but what is unseen. For what is seen is temporal, but what is unseen is eternal.[59]

For I am convinced that neither death nor life, neither angels nor demons, neither things present nor things future...nor anything in all creation, will be able to separate us from the love of God that is in Christ Jesus our Lord.[60]

[58] From the book entitled: Through the Bible through the year, by John Stott.
[59] From the book of 1 Corinthians, Chapter 4, verses 16 - 18.
[60] From the book of Romans, Chapter 8, verses 38 - 39.

EPILOGUE

I did not expect to add another section to this manuscript. My promised two years of life has expired many months ago. I had felt quite ready to leave this mortal world. I had disposed of many clothes, books, paintings and little treasures etc... and, as I have outlined, I was facing the greatest sorrow of leaving my family and friends. But here I am still! The thought of shopping and mundane stuff like that has become a real bore!

The other day a lovely young friend (by young I mean that she is in her forties, you understand) was giving me an animated account of her days. She was totally focussed on such essentials as holiday plans, daughter's graduation, repairs to the car, the dog's visit to the vet and a multitude of the daily needs of her family. All very interesting and important. But her busy life does not allow much space for what she sees as she distant future. NOW is the time that matters. Concepts like heaven and immortality do not seem to have much immediate relevance to her and they are way off her radar screen. She views me with some degree of polite incredulity if I mention my own greatly increased immobility and huge loss of energy and appetite. Obviously she does not understand that now I am so much older, little things agitate me much more than they would have done before. Sleep seems to take up the majority of my time in the day and the night. I only have to sit back and close my eyes and an hour later I wake up! This is annoying if it is during my favourite TV programme! My prayers are much less disciplined than they were, in that concentration is too tiring, but I am praying in a different way; now it feels more like I am carrying people in my heart.

One of the things that I have been wondering about recently is sometimes life seems to go on in diametrically opposite directions simultaneously. For instance, I say that I am at peace in my heart and I am aware that I am safe in my Heavenly Father's keeping, but at the same time I am feeling tremendously worried about the next session with my ophthalmologist. Peace and worry are not very comfortable bedfellows. Then the thought comes to me that Jesus himself was deeply distressed and painfully anxious in the Garden of Gethsemane about what was awaiting him. But after a while, he could say with deep commitment and absolute certain willingness in the struggles, to his heavenly father; Your will be done. *It is fairly easy to talk Christian words, but when the rubber hits the road the significance and the meaning of these words is a very different matter.* Somewhere, in what looks like confusion, there must be truth. This can be an experience at any time of our lives.

May God bless you very richly with the awareness of his love, a knowledge of his peace, and a quiet heart.

Myra Chave-Jones

Do not be anxious about anything, but in everything, by prayer and petition, present your requests to God. And the peace of God, which transcends all understanding, will guard your hearts (i.e. your emotions) and your minds (i.e your intelligence) in Christ Jesus.

Philippians Chapter 4, verses 6 and 7

About three hundred years ago John Newton wrote, what has become, a well known hymn. These words are as relevant today as they were then and they just about sums it up.

How sweet the Name of Jesus sounds
In a believer's ear!
It soothes his sorrows, heals his wounds,
And drives away his fear.

It makes the wounded spirit whole,
And calms the troubled breast;
'Tis manna to the hungry soul,
And to the weary, rest.

Dear Name, the Rock on which I build,
My Shield and Hiding Place,
My never failing treasury, filled
With boundless stores of grace!

By Thee my prayers acceptance gain,
Although with sin defiled;
Satan accuses me in vain,
And I am owned a child.

Jesus! my Shepherd, Husband, Friend,
O Prophet, Priest and King,
My Lord, my Life, my Way, my End,
Accept the praise I bring.

Weak is the effort of my heart,
And cold my warmest thought;
But when I see Thee as Thou art,
I'll praise Thee as I ought.

Till then I would Thy love proclaim
With every fleeting breath,
And may the music of Thy Name
Refresh my soul in death!

FURTHER READING

Learning to Dance	Michael Mayne
The Enduring Melody	Michael Mayne
If it isn't too Much Trouble	Anne Benson
The Cross of Christ	Rev. Dr. John Stott
The Screwtape Letters	C.S. Lewis
Mere Christianity	C.S. Lewis
Song of the Shepherd	Tony Horsfall

OTHER BOOKS BY THE SAME AUTHOR

Be Angry and Sin Not	Myra Chave-Jones, Ruth Fowke, Dick Keyes & John R.W. Stott
Coping with Depression	Myra Chave-Jones
The Gift of Helping	Myra Chave-Jones
Listening to Your Feelings	Myra Chave-Jones
Living with Anger	Myra Chave-Jones
Preparation for Marriage	Myra Chave-Jones & Sarah Howarth

PUBLISHER'S NOTE

While every effort has been made to ensure that all sources have been correctly referenced and attributed, there is always the possibility of errors. If errors of attribution subsequently come to light, they will be rectified in future reprints.

We hope that you have enjoyed reading this book. Please continue by reading the extracts of some of our other publications on the pages that follow. You can order further copies of this book, or place orders for other titles from our website at: http:///www.galacticpublishers.net/

OTHER BOOKS BY GALACTIC PUBLISHING

At Galactic Publishing we aim to bring to the market, lesser known authors, and unknown authors. As a taster for you, we have included, at the end of this book, a few extracts from some of our publications.

The first is entitled: Ouch That Hurts. This book examines the causes of the worst financial crisis since the Wall St Crash. Is it the bankers fault? Who is a Banker? Should they get such large bonuses? The author views matters of finance and wealth from a Biblical perspective, and considers whether society can bring learn any lessons from scripture. (Publication Autumn 2010)

The second extract is from a publication called: Noah and the Giraffe. This is a conversation—in the form of a series of light hearted emails— between a Christian and an Atheist! Can the Christian prove the existence of God? Can the Atheist prove that there is no God? And why does the giraffe have such a long neck? Find out the answer to all of these great questions, and many more. (Publication Summer 2010)

On our website you can also order plays in a format that is ideally suited for fund raising purposes, or just to engender community. With the scripts for each play we provide full formats of the evening suggestions, a quiz, in fact all that is required to put on a memorable evening of entertainment with little effort.

For further details, and to purchase any of our publications, please go to: http://galacticpublishers.net/

We look forward to meeting your ongoing reading pleasure needs.

Galactic Publishers Limited

Ouch!
that hurts
by Arwyn Bailey

If I were to ask you to make up a list of who you consider to be wealthy, I wonder who would make it onto your own rich list? Would any of the following be on it: Bill Gates, Richard Branson, Donald Trump, Alan Sugar, the Sultan of Brunei? Or would it be someone else entirely? How about sports stars, such as: David Beckham, Michael Jordan, Lewis Hamilton etc? What about those in showbiz, like: Simon Cowell, Cheryl Cole, Jennifer Lopez, Tom Cruise, Madonna? Perhaps you can name some other idol, or celebrity that you admire. Your list might be very long and—depending upon when you read this—it may be influenced by who is in vogue at the time.

But, what about you? Have you ever considered whether you are rich?

In order to define wealth, this book examines what we might mean by being rich, or wealthy, and what happens when it all goes horribly wrong, in what has been affectionately labelled as: The Credit Crunch.

Before you read any further I must say, in advance, that I write as a Christian and I believe that the Bible has a lot to say about the subject of wealth. As the scriptures of my faith has so much to say, it must be assumed that money and wealth is of concern to our maker. This means that we should delve and dig into the Bible in order to gain clarity, before drawing any firm conclusions.

I also believe that many of the principles outlined in the pages of the Bible, can be used by all, no matter what belief one might hold, so please do not discard this book even if you have no (or little) faith. I believe that the Holy Bible is my arbitrator, judge and jury, for I believe that it is within the pages of the Bible, ultimate truth can be discovered, and these same truths transcend history, race and culture as they are as valid for us today—and the fast paced society in which we live—as they were when they were first written.

I would like to stress that it is not my intention to make anyone feel guilty in what I write, but wealth is something that can influence us quite markedly, and it can colour our perception of one another quite significantly.

So, if you are sitting comfortably, then we will begin and let's kick off with a quote about money, wealth and fortune. The American oil magnate J.P. Getty is often cited as a man of a considerable fortune, who is quoted often. Perhaps his most famous mantra relates to his own formula for the successful acquisition of wealth. He stated that to become rich you need to:

Rise early, work hard, and strike oil.

What do you think of this statement?.........

.........no matter where you might stand on all of these issues, or how you might view the world at large, I can almost guarantee that you desire the best (however this might be defined) for: yourself; your children; and those that you love. You want a good standard of living and to be successful (however this may be defined). You like to have good holidays; live in a decent house; have a good job; and a good education must be available for yourself and for your own children. I once overheard a friend, in a moment of anger, saying to his own daughter:

If you are not careful, you will end up being a waitress, and make nothing of your life. Is that what you want to do for the rest of your life?

This father was well intentioned, but he was frustrated that his daughter had the potential to do something other than waiting at tables, which was her current part time job. He was finding it hard to motivate her into studying. But what he said reflected his innermost thoughts. He had graded the job as a waitress, as one that is lower than many others. In his eyes it was demeaning for his daughter to stoop as low as that. This same father enjoyed dining out, and when he did so he had waitresses, and waiters, in restaurants waiting upon him, naturally he would tip them. Ironically he wanted other people's daughters and sons to wait upon him, but he did not want his own daughter waiting upon others. What he was really saying to his daughter was:

If you take this path, then in my eyes you will have failed, for you will not go to university, and you will have wasted all the academic acumen that you have and you will end up in some dead end job for the rest of your life. That is failure with a big resounding 'F'.

I do not have time to go into this in too much detail, but, I am a father myself, and perhaps I am not that good a one at times, but sometimes we have to kick ourselves, and stop judging others by their occupation and the resulting level of wealth. But let me ask you a question, what would you define as being a good job? Now what would you define as a job that is detrimental and beneath you or your children? Don't say that you have never thought this way, because you probably have. Thinking about your own definitions, by categorising jobs in this manner, how do you value someone who is doing a good job? Then how do you value someone who is engaged in that other demeaning job?

Thinking out loud, would wiping the backside of someone, after they have been to the toilet be a demeaning job for you to do, or your child (and I am not talking nursing here)? Most of us would baulk at such a task. But what if I were to tell you that if you did this job, it would open up opportunities to power, wealth and influence over a nation, would that be more interesting a proposition? What if you were given a title to go with this job, say: The Groom of the Stool. Is that enough for you? Not yet? I agree with you, most would think this was the worst job that anyone could do, but allow me to put it into context. King Henry VIII had such a person, and it was not the lowest of the low who normally hankered after the job of wiping the king's bum, it was his courtiers. If you were able to do this job, you had time alone with the king, and you could become a confidante of the King, and you would have his ear on all sorts of policies. Now how does it sound?

As an example of judging people by their occupation, it is worth remembering that Einstein's early career included the evaluation of patent applications for electromagnetic at the Swiss Patent Office. But, this genius was passed over for promotion until he was able to fully master machine based technology!

Jesus was a lowly carpenter. Look what happened there.........

noah & the giraffe

by

Arwyn & Phil

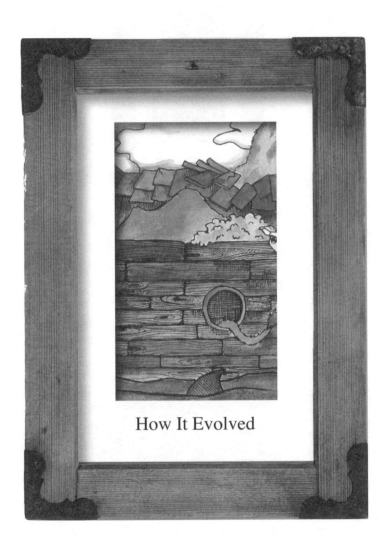

How It Evolved

The Thinker

An American monkey, after getting drunk on brandy, would never touch it again, and thus is much wiser than most men.

Charles Darwin.

For those with faith, no explanation is necessary.   For those without, no explanation is possible.

Thomas Aquinas.

Not only is there no God, but try getting a plumber on weekends.

Woody Allen.

The content presented within these pages has evolved over several months. At the outset there was certainly no intention of compiling a book. The idea just sort of happened. To some this may be inspired to others it is simply a matter of coincidence.

The result is hopefully a palatable mix of light banter and serious debate, but it is essentially two blokes just chilling out and outlining their individual viewpoints.

If anything that the authors have written offends you, please just shrug your shoulders and give the book away to someone else, or throw it in the bin.

The footnotes, that are sprinkled liberally throughout, are not essential to the reading of the conversation between the authors, but were written after the event to clarify some of the references, or the thought processes, behind the points made in the main text.

One author prays that God may be with you, the other hopes that the tendency of your genes to reproduce gives rise to more joy than grief in your life.

Arwyn & Phil.